The Science
of
GETTING
RICH

Wallace D. Wattles
and
Dr. Judith Powell

TOP OF THE MOUNTAIN PUBLISHING
Pinellas Park, Florida 33780-2244

TOP OF THE MOUNTAIN PUBLISHING
A Division of Powell Productions
P.O. Box 2244, Pinellas Park, Florida 33780-2244 U.S.A.
SAN 287-590X

CATALOG ONLINE: http://www.AbcInfo.Com
E-MAIL: rich@abcinfo.com
PHONE (727) 391-3958 * FAX (727) 391-4598

Copyright 1993 by Dr. Judith Powell
1st printing 1990 - 2nd printing 1992
3rd printing 1993 - 4th printing 1994
5th printing 1995 - 6th printing 1996
7th printing 1997 - 8th printing 1998
9th printing 1999 - 10th printing 2000
11th printing 2001 - 12th printing 2002

Library of Congress Cataloging Publication Data
Wattles, Wallace Delois
The science of getting rich / by Wallace D. Wattles and Judith L. Powell
p. cm.

ISBN 1-56087-138-5, quality pbk.: $12.95
1.Success. 2. Wealth.
I. Powell, Judith L. II. Title.
BJ1611.W3 1993 650.1'2-dc20 92-27329 CIP

Cover Design: Dr. Tag Powell
Manufactured in the United States of America

FOREWORD

*T*he challenge that faces all of us today is the universal need for money. Most of us consider that need a problem and try to treat the symptom rather than the cause. However, a small shift in our thinking allows us to see the need for money as a challenge which we can overcome on our own.

First, let us define money. Simplified, it is a medium of exchange which saves us from having to barter our goods and services. But actually, it is much more than that. Faith, hope, and trust are also a part of money, and there are many theories about its use and value. The practical and esoteric aspects of money occupy the time and talents of many people.

Here again, we will simplify — money is the teethmarks on the golden rule: "Do unto others as you would be done unto." The amount of money you get and accumulate is the measure of the service you render to others. There are other simple maxims: "Find a need and fill it;" "what goes around, comes around;" "cast your bread upon the waters." Don't get caught up in them. They seem simple, but there are myriad facets in those statements. Use them to stimulate your thinking, but not as a practice without understanding.

> *Human beings are Thinking Substance, and it takes thought, creativity, and spirit to become rich — that is, rich in physical money exchange, in mental food for thought, and rich in spiritual unfoldment of purpose.*

In order to attune yourself to the balanced "Trinity" — body, mind, and spirit; no single one of which being better or nobler than the others — you must strive to stay in the "creative" mind-set.

Central to *The Science of Getting Rich* is the theme of non-competitiveness, totally foreign to our "civilized" way of thinking. To think in terms of competition throws you into the illusionary "finite" world of limitation, thus thinking that, "there is not enough to go around."

This book will guide you to the belief and understanding that the "creative" world is "infinite," unlimited, and filled with "invisible" (to the naked eye, but not to the open mind) Form*less* Stuff. And in order to give "form" to this Formless Substance, all that is required is thinking and acting in a Certain Way.

Getting rich is as easy as being poor. And in this small book you will find a step-by-step method for becoming rich, and enjoying the advancing life — leaving the old social and religious guilts behind. If you follow these steps diligently, striving always for understanding, and monitoring your actions objectively, you will walk right into the riches you deserve. We have laid out the groundwork for you — it is up to you to use the spade.

I have revised Wattles' wording so as to facilitate your reading and flow of understanding. And have additionally added to his treatise from my own experience of teaching tens of thousands of Thinking Beings around the globe, the Universal principles, and the clarity with which to apply them.

May you receive the same abundant results as thousands of other readers have for so many decades.

In Love + Energy

Dr. Judith Powell

Dr. Judith Powell

PREFACE

*I*n writing this book I have sacrificed all considerations to plainness and simplicity of style. It is essential that certain principles be understood thoroughly, so that the accompanying methods can be applied effectively.

This book is pragmatical, not philosophical. It is a practical manual, not a textbook upon theories. It is intended for the men and women whose most pressing need is for money, who wish to get rich first and philosophize afterward. It is for those who have not found the time, means, nor opportunity to go deeply into the study of the mind, but who want results. It is for those who are willing to take the conclusions of science as a basis for action, without going into all the processes by which those conclusions were reached.

It is expected that you will take these fundamental statements upon faith, just as you would take statements concerning a law of electrical action if they were advocated by a Marconi, a Tesla, or an Edison. Having taken these statements upon faith, you will then prove their truth for yourself, as long as you act upon them without fear or hesitation.

The science applied here is an exact science, and failure is impossible. Every man or woman who does this will certainly get rich. The plan of action laid down in this book was deduced from the principles of philosophy and it has passed the supreme test of practical experiment — it works!

For the benefit of those who need a logical basis for faith, there are numerous authorities. The most basic theory on which this book's practical method is based is an ancient one — the theory that One is All, and that All is One; that One Substance manifests itself as the seemingly many elements of the material world. This single theory of the Universe is of Hindu origin, and has been gradually winning its way into the thought of the Western world for close to three hundred years. It is the foundation of all the Oriental philosophies, and of those of Descartes, Spinoza, Leibnitz, Schopenhauer, Hegel, and Emerson.

If you wish to know how the conclusions were arrived at, read the writings of Hegel and Emerson for yourself. But if you wish to reap the practical fruits of their philosophies, read this book and do exactly as it tells you to do.

Very Truly Yours
W D Wattles

Wallace Wattles

CONTENTS

CHAPTER ONE

YOU HAVE THE RIGHT TO BE RICH

*W*hatever may be said in praise of poverty, the fact remains that it is not possible to live a really complete, fulfilling, or successful life unless you are rich. You cannot rise to your greatest possible height in talent or soul development unless you have plenty of money — for to unfold the soul and to develop talent you must have many things with which to use — and you cannot have these things unless you have the money with which to buy them. It also takes

> *Your right to life means your right to have the free and unrestricted use of all the things which may be necessary to your fullest mental, spiritual, and physical unfoldment. In other words, you have a right to be rich.*

money to travel, to experience different cultures, and to further your knowledge.

You can only develop in mind, soul, and body by making use of many things, and society is currently so organized that you must have money in order to possess these things. Therefore, the basis of all advancement must be *The Science of Getting Rich*.

The object of all life is development. Everything that lives has an inalienable right to all the development for which it is capable.

Your right to life means your right to have the free and unrestricted use of all the things which may be necessary to your fullest mental, spiritual, and physical unfoldment. In other words, *you have a right to be rich.*

In this book, we will not speak of riches in a figurative way; to be really rich does not mean to be satisfied or contented with a little. No one ought to be satisfied with a little if they are capable of using and enjoying more. *The purpose of Nature is the advancement and unfolding of life.* Every individual should have all that can contribute to the power, elegance, beauty, and richness of their life — to be content with less is sinful.

The individuals who own all they want for the living of all the life they are capable of living are rich — and those who do not have plenty of money cannot have all they want. Life has advanced so far, and become so complex, that even the most ordinary man or woman requires a great amount of wealth, in order to live in a manner that even approaches completeness.

Every person naturally wants to become all that they are capable of becoming. This desire to realize innate possibilities is inherent in human nature — we cannot help wanting to be all that we can be.

Success in life means becoming what you want to be. You can become what you want to be only by making use of things — and you can have the free use of things only as you become rich enough to buy them! To understand *The*

Science of Getting Rich is, therefore, the most essential of all knowledge.

There is nothing wrong in wanting to get rich. It is not wanting money for money's sake. The desire for riches is really the desire for a richer, fuller, and more abundant life — and that desire is commendable. The person who does not desire to live more abundantly is abnormal — and the person who does not desire to have money enough to buy all they want is abnormal.

There are three motives for which we live: *1. we live for the body, 2. we live for the mind, 3. we live for the soul.* No one of these is better or holier than the other; all are equally desirable. No one of these three — body, mind, or soul — can live fully if any of the others is cut short of full life and expression. It is not right or noble to live only for the soul and deny mind or body — and it is wrong to live for the intellect and deny body and soul. It is necessary to blend and balance all three aspects of life for perfect harmony.

We are all acquainted with the serious consequences of living for the body and denying both mind and soul. And we see that real life means the complete expression of all that we can give forth through body, mind, and soul. You cannot be truly happy or satisfied unless your body is living fully in every function, and unless the same is true of your mind and your soul. Wherever there is unexpressed possibility, or purpose not performed, there is unsatisfied desire. *Desire is possibility seeking expression, or function seeking performance.*

* FACT 1. *You cannot live fully in body without good food, comfortable clothing, and warm shelter; and without freedom from excessive toil. Rest and recreation are also necessary to your physical life.*

* FACT 2. *You cannot live fully in mind without books and time to study them, without opportunity for travel and observation, nor without intellectual companionship. To live fully in mind you must have intellectual recreations, and must surround yourself with all the objects of art and beauty you are capable of using and appreciating.*

> ✳ FACT 3. To live fully in soul, you must have love; and love is denied expression by poverty. Our highest happiness is found in the bestowal of gifts to those we love – love finds its most natural and spontaneous expression in giving. If you have nothing to give, you cannot fill your place as a husband or father, wife or mother, as a citizen, or as a man or woman.

SUMMARY

It is perfectly right that you should desire to be rich; if you are a normal man or woman you cannot help doing so. It is perfectly right that you should give your best attention to *The Science of Getting Rich*, for it is the noblest and most necessary of all studies. If you neglect this study, you are derelict in your duty to yourself, to your Higher Source, and to humanity – for there is no greater service that you can give to The Source and to humanity's evolution than to *make the most of yourself*.

It is in the use of material things that we find full life for our bodies, develop our minds, and unfold our souls. It is, therefore, of supreme importance to you that you should be rich.

CHAPTER TWO

THERE IS A SCIENCE TO GETTING RICH

*T*here is a science to getting rich, and it is an exact science, like algebra or arithmetic. There are certain laws which govern the process of acquiring riches, and once you learn and obey these laws, you will get rich with mathematical certainty.

The ownership of money and property comes as a result of doing things in a *Certain Way*. Those who do things in this Certain Way, whether on purpose or accidentally, get rich; while those who do not do things in this Certain Way, no matter how hard they work or how able they are, remain poor.

It is a *natural law that like causes always produce like effects.* Therefore, any man or woman who learns to do things in this Certain Way will infallibly get rich.

That the above statement is true is shown by the following facts:

> ✳ FACT 1. *Getting rich is not a matter of environment. If it were, all the people in certain neighborhoods would become wealthy. The people of one city would all be rich, while those of other cities would all be poor; or the inhabitants of one state would roll in wealth, while those of an adjoining state (or country) would be in poverty.*

But everywhere we see rich and poor living side by side, in the same environment, and often engaged in the same vocations. When two persons are in the same locality, and in the same business, and one gets rich while the other remains poor it shows that getting rich is not primarily a matter of environment. Some environments may be more favorable than others, but when two people in the same business are in the same neighborhood, and one gets rich while the other fails, it indicates that getting rich is the result of doing things in a Certain Way.

> ✱ FACT 2. And further, the ability to do things in this Certain Way is not due solely to the possession of talent, for many people who have great talent remain poor, while others who have very little talent get rich.

Studying the people who have gotten rich, we find that they are an average lot in all respects, having no greater talents and abilities than other people. You have probably thought about this yourself — why others have "gotten ahead" in the world, who possess less talent than you, while you stay in the same old rut. It is evident that they do not get rich because they possess talents and abilities that other people don't have, but because they happen to do things in a Certain Way.

> ✳ *FACT 3. Getting rich is not the result of saving, or thriftiness. Many very miserly people are poor, while free spenders often get rich.*
>
> ✳ *FACT 4. Nor does one get rich by doing things which others fail to do; for two individuals in the same business often do almost exactly the same things, and one gets rich while the other remains poor or goes bankrupt.*

From all these things, we must come to the conclusion that getting rich is not the result of doing certain things... it is the result of doing things in a Certain Way! If getting rich is the result of doing things in a Certain Way, and if like causes always produce like effects, then any man or woman who can do things in that Way can become rich, and the whole matter is brought within the domain of exact science.

The question arises here, whether this Certain Way is so difficult that only a few may follow it. But the Certain Way, as we have seen, does not require any special natural ability. Talented people get rich, and ignoramus' get rich, and uneducated people get rich; physically strong people get rich, and weak and sickly people get rich.

Some degree of ability to think and understand is, of course, essential. But as far as natural ability is concerned, any man or woman who has sense enough to read and understand these words can certainly get rich.

Also, we have seen that it is not a matter of environment, although location counts for something — one would not go to the top of Mt. Everest, set up an ice cream parlor and expect to do successful business!

Getting rich requires dealing with people, and being where these people are. If these people are inclined to deal in the way you want to deal, so much the better. But that is about as far as environment counts.

If anybody else in your town can get rich, so can you. If anybody else in your state can get rich, so can you. If anybody else in your country can get rich, so can you!

Again, it is not a matter of choosing some particular business or profession. People get rich in every business, and in every profession, while their next-door-neighbors in the same vocation remain in poverty. It is true that you will do best in a business which you like, and which suits you. If you have developed certain talents, you will do best in a business which calls for those talents.

Also, you will do best in a business which is suited to your locality. An ice cream parlor would do better in a warm climate than in Alaska, and a salmon fishery will succeed better in the northwestern United States than in Florida, where there are no salmon!

But, aside from these general limitations, getting rich is not dependent upon your engaging in some particular business, but upon your learning to do things in a Certain Way. If you are now in business, and anybody else in your locality is getting rich in the same business, while you are not getting rich, it is because you

are not doing things in the same Way that the
other person is doing them.

> * FACT 5. *Getting rich is not a matter of*
> *lack of capital. True, as you get capital the*
> *increase becomes easier and more rapid.*
> *But one who has capital is already rich,*
> *and does not need to consider how to be-*
> *come so.*

No matter how poor you may be, when you
begin to do things in the Certain Way you will
begin to get rich; you will begin to have capital.
Getting capital is a part of the process of getting
rich. It is a part of the result which invariably
follows doing things in the Certain Way.

SUMMARY

You may be the poorest person on the con-
tinent, and be deeply in debt; you may have
neither friends, influence, nor resources. But if
you begin to do things in the Certain Way, you
must infallibly begin to get rich, for like causes
must produce like effects. If you have no capital,

you can get capital; if you are in the wrong business, you can get into the right business; if you are in the wrong location, you can go to the right location. You can do so by beginning in your *present* business and in your *present* location to do things in the Certain Way which causes success.

CHAPTER THREE

OPPORTUNITY IS AN OPEN DOOR

No man or woman is kept poor because opportunity has been taken away from them; because other people have monopolized the wealth, and have put a fence around it. You may be shut off from engaging in business in certain lines, but there are other channels open to you. Probably it would be hard for you to get control of the automobile industry; that field is pretty well monopolized. But the telecommunications industry is still booming, and offers plenty of scope for enterprise. And it will be but a very few decades until traffic and transportation through space will become a great industry, and in all its branches will employ hundreds of thousands, and perhaps millions, of people.

It is quite true that if you work as an employee of an oil company you have very little chance of becoming the owner of that company. But it is also true that if you will begin now to act in a Certain Way, you can soon leave the employ of the company; you can buy a computer and a fax, and engage in a business out of your own home. There is great opportunity at this time for people who will think, act, and work in a Certain Way.

At different periods, the tide of opportunity moves in various directions, according to the needs of the Whole, and the particular stage of social evolution which has been reached. At present, the world is setting toward telecommunications and related industries and professions. Today, opportunity is more open to the computer user more than the factory worker. It is open before the business person who supplies the computer user more than the one who supplies the factory worker; and before the professional who waits upon the computer user more than before the one who serves the working class.

There is abundance of opportunity for the person who will go with the tide, instead of trying to swim against it.

So the factory workers, either as individuals or as a class, are not deprived of opportunity. The workers are not being "kept down" by the company executives; they are not being "ground" by the trusts and conglomerates. They are where they are because they do not do things in a Certain Way.

The working class may become the master class whenever they will begin to do things in a Certain Way — the law of wealth is the same for them as it is for all others. This they must learn, or they will remain where they are as long as they continue to act as they do. The individual worker, however, is not held down by the ignorance or the mental inertia of their class. They can follow the tide of opportunity to riches, and this book will tell them how.

> *Everything you see on Earth is made from one Original Substance, out of which all things proceed. New forms are constantly being made, and older ones are dissolving; but all are shapes assumed by One Thing.*

No one is kept in poverty by a shortness in the supply of riches — there is more than enough for all! A palace as large as the Taj Mahal might be built for every family on Earth from the building material in the United States alone. And under intensive cultivation, the European community could produce wool, cotton, linen, and silk enough to clothe each person in the world finer than Solomon was arrayed in all his glory, together with food enough to feed them all abundantly. *The visible supply is practically inexhaustible; and the invisible supply really IS inexhaustible.*

Everything you see on Earth is made from one Original Substance, out of which all things proceed. New forms are constantly being made, and older ones are dissolving; but all are shapes assumed by One Thing.

There is no limit to the supply of Formless Stuff, or Original Substance. The Universe is made out of it; but it was *not* all used in making the Universe. The spaces in, through, and between the forms of the visible universe are permeated and filled with the Original Substance, with the *Formless Stuff – the raw material of all things*. Ten thousand times as much as has been made might still be made, and even then we should not have exhausted the supply of universal raw material.

No one, therefore, is poor because nature is poor, or because there is not enough to go around. *Nature is an inexhaustible storehouse of riches; the supply will never run short.* Original Substance is alive with creative energy, and is constantly producing more forms.

When the supply of building material is exhausted, more will be produced; when the soil is exhausted so that foodstuffs and materials for clothing will no longer grow upon it, the land will be renewed or more soil will be made. When all the gold and silver has been dug from the earth, if humanity is still in such a stage of social development that we need gold and sil-

> *The Formless Stuff is intelligent; it is stuff which thinks. It is alive, and is always impelled toward more life.*

ver, more will be produced from the Formless. The Formless Stuff responds to the needs of humanity; it will not let us be without anything good.

This is true of human beings collectively; the race as a whole is always abundantly rich, and if individuals are poor, it is because they do not follow the Certain Way of doing things which makes an individual rich.

The Formless Stuff is intelligent; it is stuff which thinks. It is alive, and is always impelled toward more life.

Formless Substance has the natural and inherent *impulse of life to seek to live more*. It has the nature of *intelligence* to enlarge itself, and of *consciousness* to seek to extend its boundaries, and find fuller expression. The universe of forms has been made by Formless Living Substance, throwing itself into form in order to express itself more fully.

To use the metaphor of the old *Mattel* "Vac-U-Form" toy, will give you a visual image of just how easy you can produce your needs and wants from seemingly "nothingness." The "Vac-U-Form" was a toy in which one took a sheet of plastic, which was heated then placed over a metal form (such as in the shape of a car), then drawn down by a hand pump which created a vacuum, thus molding the "formless" plastic into the shape of a car.

So too with your thinking: You take a *mental* form of your desire and "lay" it into Formless Substance (a living vacuum); and apply mental suction by thinking and acting in a Certain Way — and you have molded that which is what you desired!

SUMMARY

The Universe is a great Living Presence, always moving inherently toward more life and fuller functioning. *Nature is formed for the advancement of life*; its impelling motive is the increase of life. For this cause, everything which can possibly minister to life is bountifully provided. There can be no lack, because Higher Intelligence cannot contradict Itself and nullify Its own works.

You are not kept poor by lack in the supply of riches — it is a fact which will be demonstrated a little further on, that even the resources of the Formless Supply are at the command of the man or woman who will act and think in a Certain Way.

CHAPTER FOUR

THINKING FORM INTO EXISTENCE

*T*hought is the only power which can produce tangible riches from the Formless Substance. The stuff from which all things are made is a substance which thinks. And *the very thought of a form in this substance produces that form.*

Original Substance moves according to its thoughts; every visible form and process in nature is the expression of a thought in Original Substance. As the Formless Stuff thinks of a form, it takes that form; as it thinks of a motion, it makes that motion. That is the way all things were and are created. *We live in a thought-world, which is part of a thought-universe.*

The thought of a moving universe was extended throughout Formless Substance, and the Thinking Stuff moved according to that thought, and took the form of systems of planets.

Thinking Substance takes the form of its thought, and moves according to the thought. Holding the idea of a circling system of suns and worlds, it takes the form of these bodies, and moves them as it thinks. Thinking the form of a slow-growing oak tree, it moves accordingly, and produces the tree, though centuries may be required to do the work. In creating, the Formless seems to move according to the lines of motion it has established — the thought of an oak tree does not cause the instant formation of a full-grown tree, but it does start in motion the forces which will produce the tree, *along established lines of growth.*

Every thought of form which occurs in Thinking Substance causes the creation of the form, and this creation always takes place along the general lines of growth and action *already established.* Nature takes the line of least resistance.

> *Every thought of form which occurs in Thinking Substance causes the creation of the form, and this creation always takes place along the general lines of growth and action already established.*

Thought, when reduced down to its most basic form, is electrical in nature; electricity is energy; therefore, we can say that *thought is energy.* Energy cannot be created nor destroyed; only changed in form.

Energy was, is, and always will be. And how the energy is used or transformed is two-fold: *1. by the impression of your thought-forms; or 2. being left to pre-existing patterns (destiny).* Energy patterns can be transformed to take the shape of your thoughts, thereby freeing you from the wheel of destiny, giving you control over your fate.

The thought of a house of a certain construction, if it were impressed upon Formless Substance, might not cause the instant formation of the house, but it would turn the creative

> *No thought of form can be impressed upon Original Substance without causing the creation of the form.*

energies already working in trade and commerce into such channels as to result in the speedy building of the house. And if there were no existing channels through which the creative energy could work, then the house would be formed directly from *Primal Substance*, without waiting for the slow processes of the organic and inorganic world (Formless Substance).

No thought of form can be impressed upon Original Substance without causing the creation of the form.

You are a thinking center, and can originate thought. All the forms that you fashion with your hands must first exist in your thought. You cannot shape a thing until you have thought that thing.

And so far we have confined our efforts wholly to the work of our hands. As a society, we have applied manual labor to the world of forms, seeking to change or modify those already existing. We have never thought of trying to *cause the creation of new forms* by impressing our only thoughts upon Formless Substance!

When you have a thought-form, you take *material* from the forms of nature, and make an image of the form which is in your mind. You have, so far, made little or no effort to cooperate with Formless Intelligence; to work "with the Father." You have not dreamed that you can "do what you seeth the Father doing," as Jesus said. And that is to create with *thought*.

Humanity reshapes and modifies existing forms by manual labor; we have given no attention to the question whether we may not produce things from Formless Substance by communicating our thoughts to it. This book proposes to prove that we may do so; to prove that any man or woman may do so, and to show how. As our first step, we must lay down three fundamental propositions.

First, we assert that there is one Original Formless Stuff, or substance, from which all things are made. All the seemingly many elements are but different presentations of one element; all the many forms found in organic and inorganic nature are but different shapes,

> *There is a Thinking Stuff from which all things are made, and which, in its original state, permeates, penetrates, and fills the interspaces of the Universe. A thought in this Substance, produces the thing that is imaged by that thought. You can form things in your thoughts, and, by impressing your thoughts upon Formless Substance, can cause the thing you think about to be created.*

made from the same stuff. And this stuff is Thinking Stuff; a thought held in it produces the form of that thought. Thought, in thinking substance, produces shapes. You are a thinking center, capable of original thought; if you can communicate your thought to Original Thinking Substance, you can cause the creation, or formation, of the thing you think about. To summarize this:

There is a Thinking Stuff from which all things are made, and which, in its original state, permeates, penetrates, and fills the interspaces of the Universe. A thought in this Substance, produces the thing that is imaged by that thought. You can form things in your thoughts, and, by impressing your thoughts upon a Formless Substance, can cause the thing you think about to be created.

It may be asked if we can prove these statements; and without going into details, the answer is yes, both by logic and experience.

Reasoning back from the phenomena of form and thought, we come to one Original Thinking Substance; and reasoning forward from this thinking substance, we come to the human power to cause the formation of the thing we think about.

And by experiment, we find the reasoning true; and this is our strongest proof.

If one person who reads this book gets rich by doing what it tells them to do, that is evidence in support of our claim; and if every person who does what it tells them to do gets rich, that is positive proof, until someone goes through the process and fails. The theory is true until the process fails — and this process will not fail! Every individual who does exactly what this book tells them to do will get rich.

We have stated that you will get rich by *doing* things in a Certain Way, and in order to do so, you must become able to *think* in a Certain Way.

Your way of doing things is the direct result of the way you think about things. To do things in a way you want to do them, you will have to acquire the ability to think the way you want to think; not let your thoughts run amuck — this is the first step toward getting rich.

> * *STEP 1. To think what you want to think is to think TRUTH, regardless of appearances. Every person has the natural, inherent power to think what they want to think, and it requires far more effort to do so than it does to think the thoughts which are suggested by appearances.*

To think according to appearances is easy; to think truth regardless of appearances requires the expenditure of more power than any other work you are called upon to perform.

There is no labor from which most people shrink as they do from that of sustained and consecutive thought — it is the hardest work in the world. This is especially true when truth is contrary to appearances. Every illusion in the visible world tends to produce a corresponding form in the mind which observes it. This can only be prevented by holding the thought of the UNIVERSAL TRUTH.

To look upon the appearance of disease will produce the form of disease in your own mind, and ultimately in your body, unless you hold the thought of the truth.

* *TRUTH 1. There is no disease — it is only an illusion, and the reality is health.*

This is what Jesus did when healing the sick. He looked away from the disease, the illusion, and looked up to the heavens to focus in on the Universal Truth of health.

To look upon the appearances of poverty will produce corresponding forms in your own mind, unless you hold to the truth.

* *TRUTH 2. There is no poverty — there is only abundance.*

To think health when surrounded by the appearances of disease, or to think riches when in the midst of appearances of poverty, requires power. You must erase it from your vision; you must cancel the image from your mind; you must neutralize the thought-form and send it back to the Formless. You who acquire this power; become a MASTER MIND. You can conquer fate; you can have what you want.

This power can only be acquired by getting hold of the basic fact which is behind all appearances. *The single fact is that there is one Thinking Substance, from which and by which all things are made.*

> ✳ STEP 2. *Next, you must grasp the truth that every thought held in this substance becomes a form, and that you can so impress your thoughts upon It as to cause them to take form and become visible things.*

When you realize this, you lose all doubt and fear, for you know that you can create what you want to create. You can get what you want to have. And you can become what you want to be.

SUMMARY

As a first step toward getting rich, you must believe the three fundamental truths given previously in this chapter. For emphasis, we repeat them here.

> *1. There is a Thinking Stuff from which all things are made, and which, in its original state, permeates, penetrates, and fills the interspaces of the Universe.*
> *2. A thought in this Substance, produces the thing that is imaged by that thought.*
> *3. You can form things in your thoughts, and, by impressing your thoughts upon Formless Substance, can cause the thing you think about to be created.*

You must lay aside all other concepts of the Universe than this single one. And you must dwell upon this until it is fixed in your mind, and has become your habitual everyday thought. Read these truth statements over and over again — embed every word upon your memory, and meditate upon them until you firmly believe what they say. If a doubt comes to you, cast it aside as a sin.

Do not listen to arguments against this idea. Do not go to churches or lectures where a contrary concept is taught or preached. Do not read magazines or books which teach a different idea. Do not watch or listen to television or radio talk shows which are adverse to this central Universal theme. Do not spend time with people who espouse different viewpoints on this single idea. If you get mixed up in your faith, all your efforts will be in vain; your *thought-form will be neutralized.*

Do not ask why these things are true, nor speculate as to how they can be true; simply take them on trust. *The Science of Getting Rich* begins with the absolute acceptance of this faith.

CHAPTER FIVE

EVER-INCREASING LIFE

*Y*ou must get rid of the last vestige of the old idea that there is a Deity whose will it is that you should be poor, or whose purposes may be served by keeping you in poverty.

The Intelligent Substance which is All, and in all, and which lives in All and lives in you, is a consciously Living Substance. Being a consciously Living Substance, It must have the natural and inherent desire of moving every living intelligence toward increase of life. *Every living thing must continually seek for the enlargement of its life, because life, in the mere act of living, must increase itself.*

A seed, dropped into the ground, springs into activity, and in the act of living, produces a hundred more seeds. *Life, by living, multiplies itself.* It is forever becoming more; it must do so, if it continues to be at all.

> *Intelligence is under this same necessity for continuous increase:*
> * *Every thought we think makes it necessary for us to think another thought – consciousness is continually expanding.*
> * *Every fact we learn leads us to the learning of another fact – knowledge is continually increasing.*
> * *Every talent we cultivate brings to the mind the desire to cultivate another talent – we are subject to the urge of life, seeking expression, whichever drives us on to know more, to do more, and to be more.*

In order to know more, do more, and be more, we must have more! We must have things to use, for we learn, and do, and become, only by using things. *We must get rich, so that we can live more.*

> *The desire for riches is simply the capacity for larger life seeking fulfillment. Every desire is the effort of an unexpressed possibility to come into action.*

The desire for riches is simply the capacity for larger life seeking fulfillment. Every desire is the effort of an unexpressed possibility to come into action. It is power seeking to manifest which causes desire. That which makes you want more money is the same as that which makes the plant grow — it is LIFE, seeking fuller expression.

The One Living Substance must be subject to this inherent law of all life. It is permeated with the desire to live more; that is why it is under the necessity of creating things.

The One Substance desires to live more in you; therefore, it wants you to have all the things you can use. It is the desire of Higher Intelligence that you should get rich. It wants you to get rich because It can express Itself better through you if you have plenty of things to use in giving It expression. It can live more in you if you have unlimited command of the means of life.

The Universe desires you to have everything you want to have: Nature is friendly to your plans. Everything is naturally for you. Make up your mind that this is true.

It is essential, however, that your purpose should harmonize with the purpose that is in All.

You must want real life, not mere pleasure or sensual gratification. Life is the performance of function! And the individual really lives only when they perform every function — physical, mental, and spiritual — of which they are capable, without excess in any:

＊ *You do not want to get rich in order to live a gluttonous life, for the gratification of animal desires; that is not life. But the performance of every physical function is a part of life, and no one lives completely who denies the impulses of the body, a normal and healthful expression.*

* You do not want to get rich solely to enjoy mental pleasures, to get knowledge, to gratify ambition, to outshine others, to be famous. All these are a legitimate part of life, but the person who lives for the pleasures of the intellect alone will only have a partial life, and they will never be satisfied with their lot in life.

* You do not want to get rich solely for the good of others, to lose yourself for the salvation of humankind, to experience the joys of philanthropy and sacrifice. The joys of the soul are only a part of life; and they are no better nor nobler than any other part.

You want to get rich in order that you may:

* eat, drink, and be merry, when it is time to do these things;

* surround yourself with beautiful things, see distant lands, feed your mind, and develop your intellect;

* love others and do kind things, and be able to play a good part in helping the world to find truth.

> *You must get rid of the thought of competition. You are to create, not to compete for what is already created.*

But remember that extreme altruism is no better and no nobler than extreme selfishness; *both are excesses.*

Get rid of the idea that God or the Source wants you to sacrifice yourself for others, and that you can secure Its favor by doing so; God requires nothing of the kind. What the Infinite wants is that you should make the most of yourself, for yourself, and for others; and *you can help others more by making the most of yourself than in any other way.*

You can make the most of yourself only by getting rich; so it is right and praiseworthy that you should give your first and best thought to the work of acquiring wealth.

Remember, however, that the desire of Substance is for all, and Its movements must be for more life to all. It cannot be made to work for less life to any, because it is equally in all, seeking riches and life.

Intelligent Substance will make things for you, but it will not take things away from someone else and give them to you. You must get rid of the thought of competition. You are to create, not to compete for what is already created.

> *You are to become a creator, not a competitor! You are going to get what you want, but in such a way that when you get it, every other person will have more than they have now.*

* 1. You do not have to take anything away from anyone.
* 2. You do not have to drive sharp bargains.
* 3. You do not have to cheat, or to take advantage. You do not need to let any individual work more for you than for themselves.
* 4. You do not have to envy the property of others. No one has anything of which you cannot have, without taking anything from them.

You are to become a creator, not a competitor! You are going to get what you want, but in such a way that when you get it, every other person will have more than they have now.

It is apparent that there are people who get a vast amount of money by proceeding in direct opposition to the above statements. Tycoon-type individuals, who become very rich, do so sometimes purely by their extraordinary ability on the plane of competition. They sometimes unconsciously relate themselves to Substance in Its great purposes and movements for the general racial uplifting through industrial evolution. Rockefeller, Ford, Hughes, et. al, have been the unconscious agents of the Supreme in the necessary work of systematizing and organizing productive industry. In the end, their work has and will contribute immensely toward increased life for all.

The time for tycoons and trust magnates is nearly over. They have organized the *machinery of production*, and they will soon be succeeded by those who will organize the *machinery of distribution*.

Multi-billionaires are like the monster reptiles of the prehistoric eras — they play a necessary part in the evolutionary process, but the same Power which produced them will dispose of them. And it is well to bear in mind that they have never been really rich — a record of the private lives of most of this class will show that they have really been the most miserable and pitiful of the poor.

Riches secured on the competitive plane are never satisfactory nor permanent — they are yours today, and another's tomorrow! Remember, if you are to become rich in a scientific and Certain Way, you must rise entirely out of the competitive thought. *You must never think for a moment that the supply is limited.* Beware of the thought that all the money is being "cornered" and controlled by bankers and others, and that you must exert yourself to get laws passed to stop this process, and so on. As soon as you begin to think in that way, you drop into the competitive mind, and your power to cause creation is gone for the time being. What is worse, you will probably halt the creative movements you have already initiated.

Know that there are countless millions of dollars' worth of gold in the mountains of the earth, not yet brought to light. And *know* that if there were not, more would be created from Thinking Substance to supply your needs. *Know* that the money you need will come, even if it is necessary for a thousand people to be led to the discovery of new gold mines tomorrow.

Never look at the visible supply; *look always at the limitless riches in Formless Substance,* and *know* that riches are coming to you as fast as you can receive and use them.

SUMMARY

Nobody, by cornering the visible supply, can prevent you from getting what is yours.

* Never allow yourself to think for an instant that all the best building spots will be taken before you get ready to build your house, unless you hurry.

* Never worry about monopolies and conglomerates; never fear they will soon come to own the whole earth.

* Never be afraid that you will lose what you want because some other person "beats you to it." That cannot possibly happen; you are not seeking anything that is possessed by anyone else.

You are causing what you want to be created from Formless Substance, and the supply is without limits. Stick to the formula:

1. There is a Thinking Stuff from which all things are made, and which, in its original state, permeates, penetrates, and fills the interspaces of the Universe.

2. A thought in this Substance, produces the thing that is imaged by that thought.

3. You can form things in your thoughts, and, by impressing your thoughts upon Formless Substance, can cause the thing you think about to be created.

CHAPTER SIX

HOW RICHES COME TO YOU

*W*hen we say that you do not have to drive sharp bargains, we do not mean that you do not have to drive any bargains at all, or that you are above the need to deal with your fellow human beings. We mean that you will not need to deal with them unfairly. You do not have to get something for nothing, and you can *give to every person more than you take from them.*

You cannot give everyone more in cash market value than you take from them, but you can *give them more in use value than the cash value of the thing you get from them.* The paper, ink, and other material in this book may not be worth the money you paid for it — but if the ideas suggested in it bring you thousands of dollars, you have not been wronged by those who sold it to you. They have given you a great use value for a small cash value. Truly a win-win situation.

Let us suppose that you own a Van Gogh painting, which, in any civilized community, is worth millions of dollars. You take it to the South American Rain Forest, and by "sales skills" induce a native to collect for you plants from the Rain Forest, whose leaves contain a cancer-curing agent also worth millions of dollars on the open market, in exchange for the painting. You have really wronged him, for he has no use for the painting; it has no *use* value to him; it will not add to his life.

But suppose you give him a rifle worth $200 for his leaves; then he has made a good bargain. He has use for the rifle; it will help him to get more food; it will add to his life in every way; it will make him rich.

Give every individual more in use value than you take from them in cash value – then you are adding to the life of the world by every business transaction.

When you rise from the competitive state to the creative plane, you can scan your business transactions very strictly, and if you are selling anyone anything which does not add more to their life than the thing they give you in exchange, you can afford to stop it! You do not have to beat anybody in business. And if you are in a business which does beat people, get out of it at once.

Give every individual more in use value than you take from them in cash value – then you are adding to the life of the world by every business transaction.

If you have people working for you, you must take from them more in cash value than you pay them in wages – and you can so organize your business that it will be filled with the principle of advancement, so that each employee who wishes to do so may advance a little every day.

You can make your business do for your employees what this book is doing for you. You can so conduct your business that it will be a ladder, by which every employee who will make the effort may climb to riches themselves.

And finally, because you are to cause the creation of your riches from Formless Substance which permeates all your environment, it does not follow that they are to take shape from the atmosphere and come into being before your very eyes!

If you want an automobile, for instance, we do not mean to tell you that you are to impress the thought of an ideal car on Thinking Substance until the driving machine is formed, in the room where you sit, or elsewhere. But if you want a car, hold the mental image of it with the most positive certainty that it is being made, or is on its way to you. After once forming the thought, have the most absolute and unquestioning faith that the car is coming. Never think of it or speak of it in any other way than as being sure to arrive! Claim it as already yours. Expect to drive it.

It is like ordering from a catalog, you don't continue to look in other catalogs to order the same item; you wait for it to arrive through the mail. The natural *growth* of thought changes

If you fix upon your consciousness the fact that the desire you feel for the possession of riches is one with the desire of Omnipotence for more complete expression, your faith becomes invincible.

from how to get it to how to use it.

The car will be brought to you by the power of the Supreme Intelligence, acting upon the minds of others. If you live in Washington, it may be that a person will be brought from Michigan or Germany to engage in some transaction which will result in your getting what you want. If so, the whole matter will be as much to that person's advantage as it is to yours.

Do not forget for a moment that the Thinking Substance is through all, in all, communicating with all, and can influence all. The desire of Thinking Substance for fuller life and better living has caused the creation of all the cars already made — and it can cause the creation of millions more, and will, whenever *we set it in motion by desire and faith, and by acting in a Certain Way.*

You can certainly have an automobile in your driveway or garage. It is just as certain that you can have any other thing or things which you want, and which you will use for the advancement of your own life and the lives of others.

You need not hesitate about asking for large things: "It is your Father's pleasure to give you the kingdom," said Jesus. Original Substance wants to live all that is possible in you, and wants you to have all that you can or will use for the living of the most abundant life.

If you fix upon your consciousness the fact that the desire you feel for the possession of riches is one with the desire of Omnipotence for more complete expression, your faith becomes invincible.

Once there was a little boy sitting at a piano, vainly trying to bring harmony out of the keys. He appeared to be angry and frustrated by his inability to play real music. When asked the cause of his vexation, he answered, "I can feel the music in me, but I can't make my hands go right." The music in him was the URGE of Original Substance, containing all the possibilities of all life — all that there is of music was seeking expression through the child.

God, the One Substance, is trying to live and do and enjoy things through humanity. Supreme Intelligence is saying, "I want hands to build wonderful structures, to play divine harmonies, to paint glorious pictures. I want feet to run my errands, eyes to see my beauties, tongues to tell mighty truths and to sing marvelous songs."

All that there is of possibility is seeking expression through us. God wants those who can play music to have pianos and every other instrument, and to have the means to cultivate their talents to the fullest extent. Higher Intelligence wants those who can appreciate beauty to be able to surround themselves with beautiful things. The All wants those who can discern truth to have every opportunity to travel and observe. God wants those who can appreciate dress to be beautifully clothed, and those who can appreciate good food to be lavishly fed.

The Supreme Source wants all these things because it is the Source who enjoys and appreciates them. It is God who wants to play, and sing, and enjoy beauty, and proclaim truth, and wear fine clothes, and eat good foods. "It is God that worketh in you to will and to do," said St. Paul.

The desire you feel for riches is the Infinite, seeking to express Itself in you as It sought to find expression in the little boy at the piano.

So you need not hesitate to ask largely. Your part is to focus and express the desires of the Infinite.

This is a difficult point with most people because they retain something of the old idea that poverty and self-sacrifice are pleasing to God. They look upon poverty as a part of the plan, a necessity of nature. They have the idea that God has finished His work, and made all that He can make, and that the majority of people must stay poor because there is not enough to go around. They hold to so much of this erroneous thought that they feel ashamed to ask for wealth; they don't want more than a very modest competence, just enough to make them fairly comfortable.

In one case, a student was told that she must have in mind a clear picture of the things she desired, so that the creative thought of them might be impressed on Formless Substance.

She was a working woman, left without any assets after a divorce, and was living with a friend in a rented house. Having only what she earned from week to week, she found it difficult to grasp the fact that unlimited wealth was hers. So, after thinking the matter over, she decided that she might reasonably ask for a raise in pay so that she may help pay her friend a *fair* share of the rent.

Following the instructions given in this book, she got a *fair* pay raise within a month. It then dawned on her that she had not asked the Source for enough. She looked around her cramped surroundings, and decided that she wanted a home of her own! So she sat down with pen and paper and sketched out her ideal home: a house on the water, with large French windows opening onto a balcony, a large kitchen and dining area so she could entertain company. She made a complete picture with all the beautiful furnishings — and with herself included — and mentally impressed the thought on Formless Substance.

Holding the whole picture in her mind, she began living in the Certain Way, staying away from negative ideas contrary to the Truth, and moving toward what she wanted. After less than one year, she now owns the house (after evolving out of her low-paying job and into a high-salaried position), and she is decorating it after the form of her mental image! And now, after proving these truths to herself — and with still larger faith — she is impressing larger thoughts leading to greater things. And so it can be with you and with all of us.

SUMMARY

❋ *To be rich: you can form things in your thoughts, and, by impressing your thoughts upon Formless Substance, can cause the thing you think about to be created, and be brought into your life. In order to keep abundant living flowing, always conduct your personal and business affairs with a win-win attitude. Always give people more in use value that the cash value of the thing you get from them. Thus you will be adding to the world by working on the creative dimension rater than the competitive one.*

CHAPTER SEVEN

IS YOUR GRATITUDE SHOWING?

*T*he illustrations given in the previous chapter show that the first step toward getting rich is to convey the idea of your wants to the Formless Substance. You will see in this chapter that in order to do so *you must relate yourself to the Formless Intelligence in a harmonious way.*

To secure this harmonious relation is a matter of such vital importance that we will give you instructions which, if you will follow them,

First, you believe that there is One Intelligent Substance, from which all things proceed; second, you believe that this Substance gives you everything you desire; and third, you relate yourself to It with a feeling of deep and profound gratitude.

will be certain to bring you into perfect unity of mind with God.

The whole process of mental adjustment and attunement can be summed up in one word — *gratitude*.

First, you believe that there is One Intelligent Substance, from which all things proceed; *second*, you believe that this Substance gives you everything you desire; and *third*, you relate yourself to It with a feeling of deep and profound gratitude.

Many people who live right in all other ways are kept in poverty by their lack of gratitude. Having received one gift from God, they cut the wires which connect them with the Infinite by failing to make acknowledgment.

It is easy to understand that the nearer we live to the Source of wealth, the more wealth we will receive. And it is easy also to understand that the soul that is always grateful lives in closer touch with God than the one which never looks to the All in thankful acknowledgment. Metaphorically speaking, it's like not calling a friend to graciously thank them for a gift they sent to you.

The more gratefully we fix our minds on the Supreme when good things come to us, the more good things we will receive, and the more rapidly they will come. The reason simply is *that the mental attitude of gratitude draws the mind into closer touch with the Source from which the blessings come.*

If it is a new thought to you that gratitude brings your whole mind into closer harmony with the creative energies of the Universe, think about it, and you will see that it is true. The good things you already possess have come to you along the path of obedience to certain natural laws. *Gratitude will lead your mind to the Source of all things, keep you in close harmony with creative thought, and prevent you from falling into competitive thought.*

Gratitude alone can keep you looking toward the All, and prevent you from falling into

> *The Law of Gratitude is the natural principle that action and reaction are always equal, and in opposite directions.*

the error of thinking of the supply as limited. To think so would be fatal to your hopes.

There is a Law of Gratitude, and it is absolutely necessary that you should observe the law, if you are to get the results you want.

The Law of Gratitude is the natural principle that action and reaction are always equal, and in opposite directions.

The grateful outreaching of your mind in thankful praise to the Supreme is a liberation or expenditure of force; it cannot fail to reach That to which it is addressed, and the reaction is an instantaneous movement toward you. It is like sending a thank you note to a friend for their thoughtful gift, for which they, in turn, will acknowledge you with a return letter or a telephone call.

"Draw nigh unto God, and He will draw nigh unto you." That is a statement of psychological truth.

And if your gratitude is strong and constant, the reaction in Formless Substance will be strong and continuous — the things you want will always move toward you. Notice the grateful attitude that Jesus took, how He always seemed to be saying, "I thank Thee, Father, that Thou hearest me." You cannot exercise much power without gratitude, for it is gratitude that keeps you connected with Power.

The value of gratitude does not consist solely in getting you more blessings in the future. Without gratitude you begin to think dissatisfied thoughts regarding things as they are. The moment you permit your mind to dwell with unhappiness upon things as they are, you begin to lose ground, you fix attention upon the common, the ordinary, the poor, and the inferior. Your mind takes the form of these things. Then you will transmit these forms or mental images to the Formless — and the common, the poor, the inferior will come to you!

To permit your mind to dwell upon the inferior is to become inferior, and to surround yourself with inferior things. On the other hand,

> *The grateful mind is constantly fixed upon the best, therefore it tends to become the best; it takes the form of character of the best, and will receive the best.*

to fix your attention on the best is to surround yourself with the best, and to become the best.

The Creative Power within us makes us into the image of that on which we focus our attention. We are Thinking Substance, and thinking substance always takes the form of that which it thinks about.

The grateful mind is constantly fixed upon the best, therefore it tends to become the best; it takes the form of character of the best, and will receive the best.

Faith also is born of gratitude. The grateful mind continually expects good things, and expectation becomes faith. The reaction of gratitude upon one's own mind produces faith, and every outgoing wave of grateful thanksgiving increases faith. One who has no feeling of gratitude cannot long retain a living faith — and without a living faith you cannot get rich by the creative method.

SUMMARY

It is necessary, then, to cultivate the habit of being grateful for every good thing that comes to you, and to give thanks continuously. And because all things have contributed to your advancement, you should include all things in your gratitude.

Do not waste time thinking or talking about the shortcomings or wrong actions of corporate heads. Their organization of the world has made your opportunity; all you get actually comes to you because of them. Do not rage against corrupt politicians; if it were not for politicians we should fall into anarchy, and your opportunity would be greatly lessened.

The Supreme Intelligence has worked a long time and very patiently to bring humanity up to where we are in industry and government, and Intelligence is going right on with Its work. There is not the least doubt that God will do away with plutocrats, monopolies, and politicians as soon as they can be spared. In the meantime, be aware that they are all very good at this moment. Remember that they are all helping to arrange the lines of transmission along which your riches will come to you, so be grateful to them all. This will bring you into harmonious relations with the good in everything — and the good in everything will move toward you.

Do not worry about the seemingly negative events occurring in the world's political, environmental, and economical arenas. As societies evolve, the transitional period is the Infinite's natural way of bringing about better governments, cleaner environments, and greater use value or win-win situations.

Throughout it all, keep a clear vision of your desires, all the while knowing that no matter what new shape the world takes, your desires will be delivered to you through the existing old or new channels.

CHAPTER EIGHT

THINKING IN THE CERTAIN WAY

*T*urn back to Chapter Six, and read again the story of the woman who formed a mental image of her ideal house, and you will get a good idea of the initial step toward getting rich. That is:

> ❋ *STEP 1. You must form a clear and definite mental picture of what you want. You cannot transmit an idea unless you have it yourself, for you must have it before you can give it.*

Many people fail to impress Thinking Substance because they have only a vague and misty concept of the things they want to do, to have, or to become.

It is not enough that you should have a general desire for wealth "to do good with;" everybody has that desire! It is not enough that you should have a wish to travel, see things, live more. Everyone also has those desires. If you were going to fax a message to a friend, you would not send the letters of the alphabet in their order, and let them construct the message, nor would you take words at random from the dictionary! You would send a coherent sentence, one which meant something. When you try to impress your wants upon Substance, remember that it must be done by a coherent statement — *you must know what you want, and be definite!*

You can never get rich, or start the creative power into action, by sending out unformed longings and vague desires. Go over your desires just as the woman we've described went over her ideal house; see just what you want, and get a clear mental picture of it as you wish it to look when you get it.

You must have this clear mental picture continually in mind, as the sailor has in mind the port toward which they are sailing the ship. You must keep your face toward your picture-goal all the time. You must no more lose sight of it than the steersman loses sight of the compass.

It is not necessary to take courses in concentration, nor to set apart special times for prayer, meditation or affirmation, nor to "go into the silence," nor to do occult stunts of any kind. These things are well enough, but all you need is to know what you want, and to want it badly enough so that it will stay in your thoughts.

Spend as much of your leisure time as you can in contemplating your picture, but no one needs to take exercises to concentrate their mind on a thing which *they really want*. It is the things you do not really care about which require effort to focus your attention.

And unless you really want to get rich, so that the desire is strong enough to hold your thoughts directed to the purpose as the magnetic pole holds the needle of the compass, it will hardly be worth while for you to try to carry out the instructions given in this book. These methods set forth are for people whose desire for riches is strong enough to overcome mental laziness and the love of ease, to make them work.

The more clear and definite you make your picture, and the more you dwell upon it, bringing out all its delightful details, the stronger your desire will be. The stronger your desire, the easier it will be to hold your mind fixed upon the picture of what you want.

Something more is necessary, however, than merely to see the picture clearly. If that is all you do, you are only a dreamer, and will have little or no power for accomplishment.

* STEP 2. *Behind your clear vision must be the purpose to realize it, to bring it out in tangible expressions.*

* STEP 3. *And behind this purpose must be an invincible and unwavering faith. KNOW that the thing is already yours — that it is "coming" and you have only to take possession of it.*

Live in the new house, mentally, until it takes form around you physically. In the mental realm, enter at once into full enjoyment of the things you want. "Whatsoever things ye ask for when ye pray, believe that ye receive them, and ye shall have them," said Jesus.

> *Dwell upon your mental picture until it is clear and distinct, and then take the Mental Attitude of Ownership toward everything in the picture. Take possession of it, in mind, in the full faith that it is actually yours.*

See the things you want as if they were actually around you all the time; see yourself as owning and using them. Make use of them, as a child would, in imagination/visualization just as you will use them when they are your tangible possessions.

Dwell upon your mental picture until it is clear and distinct, and then take the *Mental Attitude of Ownership* toward everything in the picture. Take possession of it, in mind, in the full faith that it is actually yours.

Hold to this mental ownership. Do not waver for an instant in your faith that it is real!

And above all remember what was said in the preceding chapter about gratitude — be as thankful for it all the time as you expect to be when it has taken form. *The person who can sincerely thank God for the things which as yet they own only in imagination, has real faith.* They will get rich; they will cause the creation of whatever they want.

You do not need to pray repeatedly for the things you want; it is not necessary to tell God about it every day. "Use not vain repetitions as the heathen do," said Jesus to His pupils, "for your Father knoweth that ye have need of these things before ye ask Him."

Your part is to intelligently formulate your desire for the things which make for a larger life, and to get these desires arranged into a coherent whole. Then you are to impress this whole desire upon the Formless Substance, which has the power and the will to bring you what you want.

You do not make this impression by repeating strings of words. You make it by holding the vision with the unshakable INTENT of attaining it, and with the steadfast FAITH that you will attain it. Prayer is not answered according to your faith while you are talking, but according to your faith while you are *working!*

You cannot impress the mind of God by having a special Sabbath day set apart to tell Intelligence what you want, and then forgetting the Supreme during the rest of the week. You cannot impress the Source by having special hours to go into your closet and pray or meditate, if you then dismiss the matter from your mind until the hour of prayer comes again.

Verbal prayer is well enough, and has its effect, especially upon yourself, in clarifying your vision and strengthening your faith, but it is not verbal petitions which get you what you want. In order to get rich you do not need a "sweet hour of prayer;" you need to "pray without ceasing." And by prayer we mean holding steadily to your vision, with the purpose to cause its creation into solid form, and the faith that you are doing so. "Believe that ye receive them," said Jesus.

There is a joke about St. Peter opening the pearly gates for a new arrival. The man asked St. Peter, "What are all of the things, microwaves, cars, stereos — doing sitting on the clouds?" St. Peter tells him, "These are all the things people called up and ordered, but hung up the phone before we could get their address!"

SUMMARY

The whole matter turns on *receiving*, once you have clearly formed your vision. When you have formed the picture, it is well to make a verbal statement, addressing the Supreme in reverent prayer. From that moment on you must, in mind, receive what you ask for. Live in the new house; wear the fine clothes; ride in the automobile; take a plane and go on the vacation, and confidently plan for greater trips. Think and speak of all the things you have asked for in terms of actual present ownership. Imagine an environment and a financial condition exactly as you want, and live all the time in that imagined environment and financial condition. Watch, however, that you do not do this as a mere dreamer and castle builder; hold to the FAITH that the imaginary is being realized, and hold to the PURPOSE and INTENT to realize it.

Remember that it is FAITH and PURPOSE in the use of the imagination which make the difference between the scientist and the dreamer. Having learned this, you must now learn the proper use of the WILL.

CHAPTER NINE

HOW TO USE THE WILL

*T*o set about getting rich in a scientific way, you do not try to apply your will power to anything outside of yourself. You have no right to do so, anyway! It is wrong to apply your will to other men and women, in order to get them to do what you wish done.

It is as flagrantly wrong to *coerce* people by mental power as it is to coerce them by physical power. If compelling people by physical force to do things for you reduces them to slavery, com-

> *Substance is friendly to you, and is more anxious to give you what you want than you are to get it!*

pelling them by mental means accomplishes exactly the same thing. If taking things from people by physical force is robbery, then taking things by mental force is robbery also; there is no difference in principle.

You have no right to use your will power upon another person, even "for their own good," for you do not know what is for their good.

The Science of Getting Rich does not require you to apply power or force to any other person, in any way whatsoever. There is not the slightest necessity for doing so. Indeed, any attempt to use your will upon others will only defeat your purpose. You do not need to apply your will to things to make them come to you. That would simply be trying to coerce God, which would be foolish and useless, as well as irreverent.

You do not have to compel God to give you good things, any more than you have to use your will power to make the sun rise. You do not have to use your will power to conquer an unfriendly deity, or to make stubborn and rebellious forces do your bidding. Substance is friendly to you, and is more anxious to give you what you want than you are to get it!

To get rich, you need only to use your will power upon your-

> *Do not try to project your will, or your thoughts, or your mind out into space, to "act" on things or people. Keep your mind at home — it can accomplish more there than elsewhere.*

self. When you know what to think and do, then you must use your will to compel yourself to think and do the right things. That is the legitimate use of the will in getting what you want — *to use it in holding yourself to the right course.* Use your will to keep yourself thinking and acting in the Certain Way.

Do not try to project your will, or your thoughts, or your mind out into space, to "act" on things or people. Keep your mind at home — it can accomplish more there than elsewhere.

Use your mind to form a mental image of what you want, and to hold that vision with faith and purpose; and use your will to keep your mind working in the Right Way.

The more steady and continuous your faith and purpose, the more rapidly you will get rich, because you will make only POSITIVE impressions upon Substance; you will not *neutralize* or offset them by NEGATIVE impressions.

The picture of your desires, held with FAITH and PURPOSE, is taken up by the Formless, and permeates it to great distances — perhaps throughout the Universe. As this impression spreads, all things are set moving toward its realization. Every living thing, every inanimate thing, and the things not yet created, are stirred toward bringing into being that which you want. All force begins to be exerted in that direction; all things begin to move toward you. The minds of people, everywhere, are influenced toward doing the things necessary for the fulfilling of your desires; and they work for you, on an inner conscious level.

But you can put a stop to all this by starting a negative impression in the Formless Substance. DOUBT or DISBELIEF are as certain to start a movement *away* from you as FAITH and PURPOSE are to start movement *toward* you. It is misunderstanding this that causes most people who try to make use of "mental science" to fail. Every hour and moment you spend in giving thought-energy to doubts and fears, every hour you spend in worry, every hour in which your soul is possessed by disbelief, sends an *electric current* away from you in the whole domain of Intelligent Substance. All the promises are to those that believe, and to them only. Notice how insistent Jesus was upon this point of belief, and now you know the reason why.

Since belief is all important, it behooves you to guard your thoughts. As your beliefs will be shaped to a very great extent by the things you observe and think about, it is important that you control the fixation of your attention. Here the will comes into use, for it is by your will that you determine where your attention will be focused.

If you want to become rich, *you must not make a study of poverty!* Things are not brought into being by thinking about their opposites. Health is never attained by studying disease and thinking about disease; virtue is not promoted by studying sin and thinking about sin; and no one ever got rich by studying poverty and thinking about poverty.

Medicine as a science of disease has increased disease; religion as a science of sin has promoted sin; and economics as a study of poverty will fill the world with misery and want!

Do not talk about poverty — do not investigate it, or concern yourself with it. Never mind what its causes are, you have nothing to do with them. What concerns you is the cure! Do not spend your time in charitable work, or charity movements; all charity only tends to perpetuate the misery it aims to eradicate.

I do not say that you should be hard-hearted or unkind, and refuse to hear the cry of need — but you must not try to eliminate poverty in any of the conventional ways. Put poverty behind you, and put all that pertains to it behind you, and "make good."

Get rich! *The best way you can help the poor is to not be one of them.*

You cannot hold the mental image which is to make you rich if you fill your mind with pictures of poverty. Do not read books or papers, or watch television programs which give circumstantial accounts of the pitiable plight of the homeless, the hungry, of the horrors of child abuse, and so on. Do not read anything which fills your mind with gloomy images of want and suffering.

You cannot help the poor in the least by knowing about these things, and the widespread knowledge of them does not tend at all to do away with poverty, as worldwide media coverage attests. What tends to do away with poverty is not the getting of pictures of poverty into your mind, but *getting pictures of wealth into the minds of the poor!*

You are not deserting the poor in their tribulation when you refuse to allow your mind to be filled with pictures of their misery. Poverty can be done away with by increasing the number of poor people who resolve with faith to get rich, not by increasing the number of well-to-do people who think about poverty.

The poor do not need charity – they need inspiration. Charity only sends them a loaf of bread to keep them alive in their suffering, or gives them an entertaining diversion to make them forget for an hour or two. Inspiration, however, will cause them to rise out of their misery. If you want to help the poor, demonstrate to them that they can become rich — prove it by getting rich yourself!

SUMMARY

The only way in which poverty will ever be banished from this world is by getting a large and constantly increasing number of people to practice the teachings of this book.

People must be taught to become rich by creation, not by competition. Every person who becomes rich by competition throws down behind them the ladder by which they rise, and keeps others down. Every person who gets rich by creation opens a way for thousands to follow them, and inspires others to do so; and it propels the person to ever-higher rungs of the ladder.

You are not showing hardness of heart when you refuse to pity poverty, see poverty, read about poverty, think or talk about it, or listen to those who do talk about it. Use your will power to keep your mind OFF the subject of poverty, and to keep it fixed with faith and purpose ON the vision of what you want!

CHAPTER TEN

STRENGTH OF WILL LEADS TO TRUTH

*Y*ou cannot retain a true and clear vision of wealth if you are constantly turning your attention to opposing pictures, whether they be external or imaginary.

Do not tell of your past troubles of a financial nature, if you have had them — do not think of them at all. Do not tell of the poverty of your parents, or the hardships of your early life. To do any of these things is to mentally class yourself with

> *The world is not going to the devil — it is going to God. It is a wonderful Becoming.*

the poor for the time being, and it will certainly halt the movement of things in your direction.

"Let the dead bury their dead," as Jesus said. Put poverty and all things that pertain to poverty completely behind you.

You have accepted a certain theory of the Universe as being correct, and are resting all your hopes of happiness on its being correct. What can you gain by giving attention to conflicting theories?

Do not read religious books which tell you that the world is soon coming to an end. Do not read the writings of evangelists and pessimistic philosophers who tell you that it is going to the devil.

The world is not going to the devil — it is going to God. It is a wonderful Becoming.

True, there may be a good many things in existing conditions which are disagreeable. What is the use of studying them when they are certainly passing away, and when the study of them only tends to check their passing and keep them with us? Why give time and attention to things which are being removed by evolutionary growth, when you can expedite their removal only by promoting the evolutionary growth as far as your part of it goes?

No matter how horrible the conditions seem in certain places, you waste your time and destroy your own chances by considering them. You should interest yourself in the world's becoming rich. *Think of the riches the world is coming into, instead of the poverty it is growing out of.* Bear in mind that the only way in which you can assist the world in growing rich is by growing rich yourself through the creative method — not the competitive one.

Give your attention wholly to riches — ignore poverty. Whenever you think or speak of those who are poor, think and speak of them as those who are becoming rich; as those who are to be congratulated rather than pitied. Then they and others will catch the inspiration, and begin to search for the way out.

Because we say that you are to give your whole time and mind and thought to riches, it does not follow that you are to be crude or mean.

To become really rich is the noblest aim you can have in life, for it includes everything else. On the competitive plane, the struggle to get rich is a godless scramble for power over others, but when we come into the creative mind, all this is changed. All that is possible in the way of service and lofty endeavor, of greatness and the unfolding of the soul, comes by way of getting rich — all is made possible by the use of things.

If you lack for physical health, you will find that the attainment of it is conditional on your getting rich. Only those who are freed from financial worry, and who have the means to live a carefree existence and follow hygienic practices, can have and retain health.

Moral and spiritual greatness is possible only to those who are above the competitive battle for existence. Only those who are becoming rich on the plane of creative thought are free from the degrading influences of competition.

If your heart is set on domestic happiness, remember that love flourishes best where there is refinement, a high level of thought, and free-dom from corrupting influences — and these are to be found only where riches are attained by the exercise of creative thought, without stress or rivalry.

You can aim at nothing so great or noble, we repeat, as to become rich! And you must fix your attention upon your mental picture of riches, to the exclusion of all that may tend to dim or obscure the vision.

You must learn to see the underlying TRUTH in all things. You must pull back the veil, and dispel the illusion. You must see beneath all seemingly wrong conditions to the Great One Life, ever growing toward fuller expression and more complete happiness.

It is the truth that there is no such thing as poverty; that there is only wealth.

* 1. Some people remain in poverty because they are ignorant of the fact that there is wealth for them. These facts can best be taught by showing others the way to affluence in your own personal life.

✸ 2. Others are poor because, while they feel that there is a way out, they are too intellectually lethargic to put forth the mental effort necessary to find that way and travel it. For these people the very best thing you can do is to arouse their desire by showing them the happiness that comes from being rightly rich.

✸ 3. Others still are poor because, while they have some notion of science, they have become so swamped and lost in the maze of metaphysical and occult theories that they do not know which road to take. They try a mixture of many systems and fail in all. For these, again, the very best thing to do is to show the right way in your own person and practice. An ounce of doing things is worth a pound of theorizing!

The very best thing you can do for the whole world is to make the most of yourself. You can serve God and humanity in no more effective way than by getting rich — that is, if you get rich by the creative method, and not by the competitive one.

We assert that this book gives in detail the principles of *The Science of Getting Rich*, and if that is true, you do not need to read any other book upon the subject, unless it is complementary to these ideas. This may sound narrow and egotistical, but consider: there is no more scientific method of computation in mathematics than by addition, subtraction, multiplication, and division; no other method is possible. There can be but one shortest distance between two points. There is only one way to think scientifically, and that is to think in the way that leads by the most direct and simple route to the goal. No one has yet formulated a briefer or less complex "system" than the one set forth here. It has been stripped of all non-essentials. When you embark on this journey, put all others aside; erase them out of your mind altogether.

Read this book every day; keep it with you; commit it to memory, and do not think about other "systems" and theories. If you do, you will begin to have doubts, and to be uncertain and wavering in your thought. You will then begin to make failures.

After you have made good and become rich, you may study other systems as much as you please; but until you are quite sure that you have gained what you want, do not read anything on this line but this book, except for works by the authors mentioned in these pages.

And read only the most optimistic comments on the world's news, those in harmony with your picture. Also, postpone your investigations into the occult. Do not dabble in Theosophy, Spiritualism, or like studies. It is very likely that the dead still live, and are near — but if they are, let them alone; mind your own business. Just because they're dead doesn't mean they're smart!

Wherever the spirits of the dead may be, they have their own work to do, and their own problems to solve. We have no right to interfere with them. We cannot help them, and it is very doubtful whether they can help us, or whether we have any right to trespass upon their time if they can. Let the dead and the hereafter alone, and solve your own problem — get rich. If you begin to mix with the occult, you will start mental cross-currents which will surely bring your hopes to ruin.

SUMMARY

Now, this and the preceding chapters have brought us to the following statement of basic truths:

1. There is a Thinking Stuff from which all things are made, and which, in its original state, permeates, penetrates, and fills the interspaces of the Universe.

2. A thought in this Substance, produces the thing that is imaged by that thought.

3. You can form things in your thoughts, and, by impressing your thoughts upon Formless Substance, can cause the thing you think about to be created.

4. *In order to do this, you must pass from the competitive to the creative mind. You must form a clear mental picture of the*

> *things you want. Hold this picture in your thoughts with the fixed PURPOSE to get what you want, along with the unwavering FAITH that you do get what you want. Close your mind against all that may tend to shake your purpose, dim your vision, or abate your faith.*

In addition to all this, we will now see that you must live and act in the Certain Way.

CHAPTER ELEVEN

ACTING IN THE CERTAIN WAY

*T*hought is the creative power, or the impelling force which causes the creative power to act. Thinking in a Certain Way will bring riches to you, but you must not rely upon thought alone, paying no attention to personal action. That is the rock upon which many otherwise scientific metaphysical thinkers meet disaster — the failure to *connect thought with personal action.*

We have not yet reached the state of development, even supposing such a stage to be possible, in which we can create directly from Formless Substance (or Primal Stuff) without nature's processes or the work of human hands. *We must not only think, but our personal action must supplement our thoughts.*

By thought you can cause the gold in the hearts of the mountains to be impelled toward you — but it will not mine itself, refine itself, coin itself into Krugerrands, and come rolling along the roads seeking its way into your pocket!

Under the impelling power of the Supreme Spirit, humanity's affairs will be so ordered that someone will be led to mine the gold for you. Other business transactions will be so directed that the gold will be brought toward you, and you must so arrange your own business affairs that you may be able to receive it when it comes to you.

The Science of Getting Rich is being at the right place of THOUGHT... at the right time of ACTION... with the right grateful ATTITUDE.

Your thought makes all things, animate and inanimate, work to bring you what you want — and your personal activity must be such that you can rightly receive what you want when it reaches you. You are not to take it as charity, nor to steal it. You must give every person more in use value than they give you in cash value.

The scientific use of thought consists:

1. in forming a clear and distinct MENTAL IMAGE of what you want;

2. in holding fast to the PURPOSE to get what you want; and

3. in realizing with grateful FAITH that you do get what you want.

Do not try to "project" your thought in any mysterious way, with the idea of having it go out and do things for you. That is wasted effort, and will weaken your power to think with sanity.

The action of thought in getting rich is fully explained in the preceding chapters. Your faith and purpose positively impress your vision upon Formless Substance (almost like the vacuum-forming of plastics), which has THE SAME DESIRE FOR MORE LIFE THAT YOU HAVE. *This vision, received from you, sets all the creative forces at work in and through their regular channels of action, and directs them toward you.*

It is not your part to guide or supervise the creative process — all you have to do with that is to *1. retain your vision, 2. stick to your purpose, 3. and maintain your faith and gratitude. And 4. you must act in a Certain Way,* so that you can appropriate what is yours when it comes to you; so that you can meet the things you have in your picture, and put them in their proper places as they arrive.

You can readily see the truth of this. When things reach you, they will be in the hands of other people, who will ask for an equivalent payment for them. And you can only get what is yours by giving the other person what is theirs. Your wallet or purse is not going to be transformed into a Fortunate's purse, which will be always full of money without effort on your part.

This is the crucial point in *The Science of Getting Rich:* right here, where *thought and personal action must be combined.* There are very many people who, outer consciously or inner consciously, set the creative forces in action by the strength and persistence of their desires,

and who still re-
main poor because
they do not provide
for the *reception* of
the thing they want

> *By thought, the thing you want is brought to you; by action you receive it.*

when it comes! They think or wish for things, never *expecting* to receive them — they do not provide room or space in their life for these things.

(Highly recommended reading to help you combine thought with personal action is *Think Wealth... Put Your Money Where Your Mind Is!* by Dr. Tag Powell. Whereas our book inspires the mind and spirit, Powell's book motivates the body into action by thought. Available through this publisher.)

By thought, the thing you want is brought to you; by action you receive it. Whatever your action is to be, it is evident that *you must act NOW. You cannot act in the past,* and it is essential to the clearness of your mental vision that you dismiss the past from your mind. *You cannot act in the future,* for the future is not here yet. And you cannot tell how you will want to act in any future contingency until that contingency has arrived.

Because you are not in the right business, or the right environment now, do not think that you must postpone action until you get into the right business or environment. And do not spend time in the present thinking about the best course in possible future emergencies. *Have faith in your ability to meet any emergency when it arrives!*

If you act in the present with your mind on the future, your present action *will be with a divided mind*, and will not be effective. *Put your whole mind into present action.*

Do not give your creative impulse to Original Substance, and then sit down and wait for results. If you do this, you will never get them. Act now!

You cannot act where you are not; you cannot act where you have been; and you cannot act where you are going to be. You can act only where you are.

✸ Do not bother as to whether yesterday's work was well done or poorly done. Do today's work well.

* Do not try to do tomorrow's work now; there will be plenty of time to do that when you get to it.
* Do not try, or mystical means, to act on people or things that are out of your reach.
* Do not wait for a change of environment before you act — get a change of environment by action.

You can so act upon the environment in which you are now, as to cause yourself to be transferred to a better environment. Hold with FAITH and PURPOSE the vision of yourself in the better environment, and act upon your present environment with all your heart, and with all your strength, and with all your mind. Do not spend any time in daydreaming or castle-building. Hold to the one vision of what you want, and act NOW.

Do not mull around seeking some new thing to do, or some strange, unusual, or remarkable action to perform as a first step toward getting rich. Your actions, at least for some time to come, will probably be those you have been performing for some time past. Only now you begin to perform these actions in the Certain Way, which will surely make you rich.

If you are engaged in some business, and feel that it is not the right one for you, do not wait until you get into the right business before you begin to act. Do not feel discouraged, or sit down and brood because you are misplaced. No one was ever so misplaced that they could not find the right place, and no one ever became so involved in the wrong business that they could not get into the right business.

Hold the vision of yourself in the right business, with the INTENT to get into it, and the FAITH that you will get into it, that you are getting into it — and ACT in your present business. Use your present business as the means of getting a better one, and use your present environment as the means of getting into a better one. Your vision of the right business, if held with faith and purpose, will cause the Supreme to move the right business toward you. Your action, if performed in the Certain Way, will cause you to move toward the right business.

If you are an employee, or wage-earner, and feel that you must change places in order to get what you want, do not "project" your thoughts into space and rely upon them to get you another job. It will probably fail to do so.

Hold the VISION of yourself in the job you WANT, while you ACT with FAITH and PURPOSE on the job you have, and you will certainly get the job you want. Your VISION and FAITH will set the creative force in motion to bring it toward you, and your ACTION will cause the forces in your own environment to *propel* you toward the place you want.

SUMMARY

There is never any time but now, and there never will be any time but now. If you are ever to begin to make ready to receive what you want, you must begin now. Your action, whatever it is, will most likely be in your present business or employment, and must be upon the persons and things in your present environment.

In closing this chapter, we will add another truth to our summary:

1. There is a Thinking Stuff from which all things are made, and which, in its original state, permeates, penetrates, and fills the interspaces of the Universe.

2. A thought in this Substance produces the thing that is imaged by that thought.

3. You can form things in your thoughts, and, by impressing your thoughts upon Formless Substance, can cause the thing you think about to be created.

4. In order to do this, you must pass from the competitive to the creative mind. You must form a clear mental picture of the things you want. Hold this picture in your thoughts with the fixed PURPOSE to get what you want, along with the unwavering FAITH that you do get what you want. Close your mind against all that may tend to shake your purpose, dim your vision, or abate your faith.

5. *That you may receive what you want when it comes, you must act NOW upon the people and things in your present environment.*

CHAPTER TWELVE

EFFICIENT DAILY ACTION

*Y*ou must use your thought as directed in previous chapters, and begin to do what you can do where you are; and you must do ALL that you can do where you are.

You can advance only by being *larger* than your present place; and no one can be larger than their present place as long as they leave undone any of the work pertaining to that place.

The world is advanced only by those who *more than fill* their present places. If no one

Social evolution is guided by the law of physical and mental evolution — advancement through largeness of life.

quite filled their present place, you can see that everything must be going backward. Those who do not quite fill their present places are a dead weight upon society, government, commerce, and industry. They must be carried along by others at a great expense. The progress of the world is retarded only by those who do not fill the places they are holding. They belong to a former age and a lower plane of life, and their tendency is toward degeneration. No society could advance if every person was smaller than their place — *social evolution is guided by the law of physical and mental evolution — advancement through largeness of life.*

In the animal world, evolution is caused by excess of life. When an organism has more life than can be expressed in the functions of its own plane, it develops the organs of a higher plane, and a new species is originated. There never would have been new species had there not been organisms which more than filled their places. The law is exactly the same for you — your getting rich depends upon your applying this evolutionary principle to your own affairs.

> *You cannot foresee the results of even the most trivial act. You do not know the workings of all the forces that have been set moving in your behalf.*

Every day is either a successful day or a day of failure — and it is the successful days which get you what you want. If every day is a failure, you can never get rich, while if every day is a success, you cannot fail to get rich. If there is something that may be done today, and you do not do it, you have failed in so far as that thing is concerned — and the consequences may be more disastrous than you imagine!

You cannot foresee the results of even the most trivial act. You do not know the workings of all the forces that have been set moving in your behalf. Much may depend on your doing some simple act — it may be the very thing which is to open the door of opportunity to great possibilities. You can never know all the combinations which Supreme Intelligence is

It is really not the number of things you do, but the EFFICIENCY of each separate action that counts!

making for you in the world of things and of human affairs. *Your neglect or failure to do some small thing may cause a long delay in getting what you want.*

Do, every day, ALL that can be done that day. There is, however, a limitation or qualification of the above that you must take into account. *You are not to overwork, nor to rush blindly into your business in the effort to do the greatest possible number of things in the shortest possible time.* You are not to try to do tomorrow's work today, nor to do a week's worth of work in a day.

It is really not the number of things you do, but the EFFICIENCY of each separate action that counts!

* *Every act is, in itself, either a success or a failure.*
* *Every act is, in itself, either efficient or inefficient.*

❋ *Every inefficient act is a failure, and if you spend your life in doing inefficient acts, your whole life will be a failure.*

The more things you do, the worse for you, if all your acts are inefficient ones. On the other hand, every efficient act is a success in itself, and if every act of your life is an efficient one, your whole life MUST be a success.

The cause of failure is doing too many things in an inefficient manner, and not doing enough things in an efficient manner. You will see that it is a self-evident proposition that if you do not do any inefficient acts, and if you do a sufficient number of efficient acts, you will become rich. If, now, it is possible for you to make each act an efficient one, you see again that the getting of riches is reduced to an exact science, like mathematics.

It is *the Law of Averages*. Remember that the majority rules, so all you need to do is to increase your efficiency rate to 51%! The matter turns, then, on the question whether you can make each separate act a success in itself. And this you can certainly do. You can make each

> *Every act can be made strong and efficient by holding your VISION while you are doing it, and putting the whole power of your FAITH and PURPOSE into it.*

act a success, because All Power is working with you; and All Power cannot fail. Power is at your service, and to make each act efficient you have only to put power into it.

Every action is either strong or weak, and when every act is strong, you are acting in the Certain Way which will make you rich. *Every act can be made strong and efficient by holding your VISION while you are doing it, and putting the whole power of your FAITH and PURPOSE into it. We call this THE POINT OF POWER.*

It is at this point that people fail who separate mental power from personal action. They use the power of mind in one place and at one time, and they act in another place and at another time. So their acts are not successful in themselves — too many of them are inefficient. But *if All Power goes (body, mind, and spirit) into every act, no matter how commonplace, every act will be a success in itself.* As in the nature of

things, every suc-
cess opens the way
to other successes,
your progress to-
ward what you
want, and the pro-
gress of what you
want toward you,
will become increa-
singly rapid.

> *It is at this point that people fail who separate mental power from personal action. They use the power of mind in one place and at one time, and they act in another place and at another time.*

Remember that *successful action is cumulative in its results — it builds momentum.* Since the desire for more life is inherent in all things, when you begin to move toward larger life more things *attach* themselves to you, and the influence of your desire is multiplied.

Do, every day, all that you can do that day, and do each act in an efficient manner. In saying that you must hold your vision while you are doing each act, however trivial or commonplace, it is not necessary at all times to see the vision distinctly in its smallest details. It should be the work of your leisure hours to use your visions, and to contemplate them until they are firmly fixed upon your memory. If you wish speedy results, spend practically all your spare time in this practice.

By continuous contemplation you will impress the picture of what you want, even to the smallest details, firmly upon your mind. And the picture will be so completely transferred to the mind of Formless Substance, that in your working hours you need only to mentally refer to the picture (like a mental photograph) to stimulate your faith and purpose, and trigger your best effort to be put forth.

SUMMARY

Efficient action means to think of your vision or goal while you are taking action on everyday matters. Think to yourself, "I am doing this action so as to bring this goal-oriented result."

Contemplate your picture in detail during your leisure hours until your consciousness is so filled with it that you can grasp it instantly. You will become so infused with its bright promises that the mere thought of it will call forth the strongest energies and emotions of your whole being.

Let us again repeat our summary truths, and by adding one more statement, bring it to the point we have now reached:

1. There is a Thinking Stuff from which all things are made, and which, in its original state, permeates, penetrates, and fills the interspaces of the Universe.

2. A thought in this Substance produces the thing that is imaged by that thought.

3. You can form things in your thoughts, and, by impressing your thoughts upon Formless Substance, can cause the thing you think about to be created.

4. In order to do this, you must pass from the competitive to the creative mind. You must form a clear mental picture of the things you want. Hold this picture in your thoughts with the fixed PURPOSE to get what you want, along with the unwavering FAITH that you do get what you want. Close your mind

against all that may tend to shake your purpose, dim your vision, or abate your faith.

5. That you may receive what you want when it comes, you must act NOW upon the people and things in your present environment.

6. *You must do, with FAITH and PUR-POSE, ALL that can be done each day, doing each separate thing in an EFFI-CIENT MANNER.*

CHAPTER THIRTEEN

GETTING INTO THE RIGHT BUSINESS

*S*uccess, in any particular business, depends upon your possessing, in a well-developed state, the faculties required in that business.

Without a good musical faculty no one can
succeed as a teacher of music; without well-
developed mechanical faculties no one can
achieve great success in any of the mechanical
trades; without tact and the commercial faculties no one can succeed in a sales career. But to

possess, in a well-developed state, the faculties required in your particular vocation does not ensure your getting rich. There are musicians who have remarkable talent, and yet remain poor; there are mechanics, builders, technicians, computer experts, and so on who have excellent dexterous skills, but who do not get rich; and there are merchants with good faculties for dealing with people who nevertheless fail.

The different faculties are tools: it is essential to have good tools, but it is also *essential that the tools be used in the Right Way*. One individual can take a sharp saw, a square, a good plane, and so on, and build a beautiful piece of furniture; another person can take the same tools and set to work to duplicate the piece, but produce a failure. They do not know how to use good tools in a successful way.

The various faculties of your mind are the tools with which you must do the work which is to make you rich. It will be easier for you to succeed if you get into a business for which you are well-equipped with the specific mental tools.

Generally speaking, you will do best in that business which will use your strongest faculties;

the one for which you are naturally "best-fitted." But there are limitations to this statement. No one should regard their vocation as being irrevocably fixed by the tendencies with which they were born.

> *You will get rich most easily in terms of effort, if you do that for which you are best-suited, but you will get rich most satisfactorily if you do that which you WANT to do.*

You can get rich in ANY business; *if you don't have the right talent for it, you can develop that talent.* It merely means that you will have to make your tools as you go along, instead of confining yourself to the use of those with which you were born. It will be EASIER for you to succeed in a vocation for which you already have the talents in a well-developed state; but you CAN succeed in any vocation, for you can develop any rudimentary talent, and there is no talent of which you have not at least the basics.

You will get rich most easily in terms of effort, if you do that for which you are best-suited, but you will get rich most satisfactorily if you do that which you WANT to do.

Doing what you want to do is life — there is no real satisfaction in living if we are compelled to be forever doing something which we do not like to do, if we can never do what we want to do. The will to live, in such circumstances, is extinguished, and many individuals die at a young age. It is certain that you can do what you want to do; the desire to do it is proof that you have within you the power which *can do it!*

Desire is a manifestation of power. The desire to play music shows that the power which can play music is seeking expression and development through you; the desire to invent mechanical devices is the mechanical talent seeking expression and development through you.

Where there is no power, either developed or underdeveloped, to do a thing, there is never any stirring to do that thing. Where there is strong desire to do a thing, it is certain proof that the power to do it is strong, and only requires to be developed and applied in the Right Way.

All other things being equal, it is best to select the business for which you have the best-developed talent. And if you have a strong desire to engage in any particular line of work, you should select that work as the ultimate end at which you aim. You can do what you want to do, and it is your right and privilege to follow the business or avocation which will be most congenial and pleasant. You are not obliged to do what you do not like to do, and should not do it, except as a means to bring you to the doing of the thing you want to do.

If there are past mistakes whose consequences have placed you in an undesirable business or environment, you may be obliged for some time to do what you do not like to do. You can, however, make the doing of it pleasant by knowing that it is allowing you to come to the doing of what you want to do.

If you feel that you are not in the right vocation, do not act too hastily in trying to get into another one. The best way, generally, to change business or environment is by growth. However, do not be afraid to make a sudden and radical change if the opportunity is presented, and you feel, after careful consideration, that it is the right opportunity. *Never take*

> *When you are in doubt, wait. Fall back on the contemplation of your vision, and increase your faith and purpose.*

sudden or radical action when you are in doubt as to the wisdom of doing so.

There is never any hurry on the creative plane – and *there is no lack of opportunity.* When you get out of the competitive mind you will understand that you never need to act hastily. No one else is going to beat you to the thing you want to do; there is enough for all! If one place is taken, another and a better one will be opened for you a little farther on; there is plenty of time. When you are in doubt, wait. Fall back on the contemplation of your vision, and increase your faith and purpose. *By all means, in times of doubt and indecision, cultivate gratitude.*

A day or two spent in contemplating the vision of what you want, and in giving earnest thanks that you are getting it, will bring your mind into such close relationship with the Supreme that you will make no mistake when you do act. There is a Mind which knows all there is to know, and you can come into very close unity with this mind by faith and the purpose to advance in life, if you have deep GRATITUDE.

> *Mistakes come from acting hastily, or from acting in fear or doubt, or in forgetfulness of the Right Motive. Remember: More life to all, and less to none.*

Mistakes come from acting hastily, or from acting in fear or doubt, or in forgetfulness of the Right Motive. Remember: More life to all, and less to none.

SUMMARY

As you go on in the Certain Way, opportunities will come to you in increasing number. You will need to be very steady in your FAITH and PURPOSE, and to keep in close touch with the All Mind by reverent GRATITUDE. Do all that you can do in a perfect manner every day, but do it without haste, worry, or fear. Go as fast as you can, but never hurry.

Remember that in the moment you begin to hurry, you cease to be a creator and become a competitor — you drop back upon the old plane again. Whenever you find yourself hurrying, call a halt. Focus your attention on the mental image of the thing you want, and begin to give thanks that you are getting it. The exercise of GRATITUDE will not fail to strengthen your FAITH, and renew your PURPOSE.

CHAPTER FOURTEEN

THE IMPRESSION OF INCREASE

*W*hether you change your vocation or not, your actions for the present must be those pertaining to the business in which you are now engaged.

You can get into the business you want by making constructive use of the business you are already established in — by doing your daily work in the Certain Way. And in so far as your business consists of dealing with other people, whether personally or by letter, the key-thought

> *The Law of Perpetual Increase: The desire for increase is inherent in all nature; it is the fundamental impulse of the Universe.*

of all your efforts must be to convey to their minds the impression of increase.

Increase is what all men and all women are seeking. It is the urge of the Formless Intelligence within us, seeking fuller expression. *The desire for increase is inherent in all nature; it is the fundamental impulse of the Universe.* All human activities are based on the desire for increase: people seek more food, more clothes, better housing, more luxury, more beauty, more knowledge, more pleasure — increase in something, everything — increase in life!

Every living thing needs this continuous advancement. Where increase of life ceases, dissolution and death set in at once. You see death set in on some people when they "retire" from a job — they have no vision to take its place.

This *Law of Perpetual Increase* is explained by Jesus in the parable of the talents: only those who gain more, retain any; from those who have not, it will be taken away even that which they have. Humans instinctively know this, and so we are forever seeking more.

The normal desire for increased wealth is not an evil or a reprehensible thing, it is simply the desire for more abundant life — it is aspiration. And because it is the deepest instinct of their natures, all men and women are attracted to those who can give them more of the means of life.

In following the Certain Way as described in the previous pages, you are getting continuous increase for yourself, and you are giving it to all with whom you deal. *You are a creative center, from which increase is given off to all.*

Be sure of this, and convey assurance of this fact to every man, woman, and child with whom you come in contact. No matter how small the transaction, even if it be only the selling of a bag of bread, put into it the thought of increase, and make sure that the customer is impressed with the thought.

Convey the impression of advancement with everything you do, so that all people will receive the impression that you are an *Advancing Hu-*

man, and that you advance all who deal with you. Give the thought of increase even to the people whom you meet socially, without any thought of business, and to whom you do not try to sell anything.

You can convey this impression by holding the unshakable faith that you, yourself, are in the Way of Increase, and by letting this faith inspire, fill, and permeate every action. *Do everything that you do in the firm conviction that you are an advancing personality, and that you are giving advancement to everyone.* Feel that you are getting rich, and that in so doing you are making others rich, and conferring benefits on all.

Do not boast or brag of your success, or talk about it unnecessarily – true faith is never boastful.

Wherever you find a boastful person, you find one who is secretly doubtful and afraid. Simply feel the faith, and let it work out in every transaction. Let every act and manner and look express the quiet assurance that you are getting rich — that you are *already* rich. Words will not be necessary to communicate this feeling to others. They will feel the sense of increase when in your presence, and will be attracted to you again.

You must so impress others that they will feel that in associating with you they will get increase for themselves. See that you give them a use value greater than the cash value you are taking from them.

Take an honest pride in doing this and let everybody know it; and you will have no lack of customers. People will go where they are given increase. The Supreme, which desires increase in all, and which knows all, will move toward you, men and women who have never heard of you. Your business will increase rapidly, and you will be surprised at the unexpected benefits which will come to you. You will be able from day to day to make larger combinations, secure greater privilege, and to go on into a more congenial vocation if you desire to do so.

But in doing all this, you must never lose sight of your vision of what you want, or your faith and purpose to get what you want.

Another word of caution in regard to motives: Beware of the deceitful temptation to seek for power over others. Nothing is so pleasant to the unformed or partially developed mind as the exercise of power or dominion over others. The desire to rule for selfish gratification has been the curse of the world. For countless ages, kings and lords have drenched the earth with blood in their battles to extend their dominions; not to seek more life for all, but to get more power for themselves.

Today, the main motive in the business and industrial world is the same: groups marshal their armies of dollars, and lay waste the lives and hearts of millions in the mad scramble for power over others. Commercial kings, like political kings, are inspired by the lust for power.

Jesus saw this desire for mastery as the motivating impulse of that corrupt world He sought to overthrow. Read the *twenty-third chapter of Matthew,* and see how He pictures the lust of the Pharisees to be called "Master," to sit in high places, to domineer over others, and to lay burdens on the backs of the less fortunate. Note how He compares this lust for dominion with the brotherly seeking for the Common Good to which He calls His disciples.

SUMMARY

To be better than another human, animal, thing is the Right Way to lead you toward increase and advancement. It is increase life and advancement for ALL.

Look out for the temptation to desire authority, to become a "master," to be considered as one who is above the common herd, to impress others by lavish display, and so on.

The mind that seeks for mastery over others is the competitive mind; and the competitive mind is not the creative mind. In order to master your environment and your destiny, it is not at all necessary that you should rule over your fellow human beings. Indeed, when you fall into the world's struggle for the high places, you begin to be conquered by fate and environment, and your getting rich becomes a matter of chance and speculation. Be secure within yourself; take care of your own business, and leave others to theirs. You can only guide by example — get rich using the creative mind.

Beware of the competitive mind! No better statement of the principle of creative action can be formulated than the renewed Golden Rule: "What I want for myself, I want for everyone."

CHAPTER FIFTEEN

THE ADVANCING HUMAN

*W*hat we stated in the previous chapter applies to the professional as well as the wage-earner and business-owner.

No matter whether you are a physician, a teacher, or a religious, if you can give increase of life to others and make them sensible of the fact, they will be attracted to you, and you will get rich. The physician who holds the vision of themselves as a great and successful healer, and who works toward the complete realization of that vision with faith and purpose, as described in former chapters, will come into such close touch with the Source of Life that they will be phenomenally successful. Patients will come to them in throngs.

No one has a greater opportunity to carry into effect the teachings of this book than the practitioner of medicine. It does not matter to which of the various schools they may belong, for the principle of healing is common to all of them, and may be reached by all alike. The Advancing Human in medicine, who holds to a clear mental image of themselves as successful, and who obeys the laws of faith, purpose, and gratitude, will cure every curable case they undertake, no matter what remedies they may use.

In the field of religion, the world cries out for the religious person who can teach their followers the true science of abundant life. Those who master the details of *The Science of Getting Rich*, together with the allied sciences — *The Science of Being Healthy*, and *The Science of Becoming Excellent* — and who teach these details from the pulpit, will never lack for a congregation. This is the gospel that the world needs! It will give increase of life, and people will hear it gladly, and will give liberal support to those who bring it to them.

What is now needed is a demonstration of the *science of life* from the pulpit. We want preachers who cannot only tell us how, but can *show* us how, by the example of their own persons. We need the preacher, or minister, who will themselves be rich, healthy, excellent, and beloved, to teach us how to attain to these things.

The same is true of the teacher who can inspire children with the faith and purpose of the advancing life. They will never be "out of a job." Any teacher who has this faith and purpose can truly give to their pupils. They cannot help giving it to them if it is part of their own life and practice.

What is true of the teacher, preacher, and physician is true of the lawyer, dentist, realtor, banker — it is true of everyone.

The combined mental and personal action we have described is infallible. Every man and woman who follows these instructions consistently, patiently, and to the letter, will get rich.

> *Do all the work you can do, every day, and do each piece of work in a perfectly successful manner. Have the purpose to get rich, and put the power of success, in everything that you do.*

The *Law of the Increase of Life* is as mathematically certain in its operation as the law of gravitation.

The wage-earner will find this as true of their case as of any of the others mentioned. Do not feel that you have no chance to get rich because you are working where there is no visible opportunity for advancement, where wages are small and the cost of living high. Form your clear mental vision of what you want, and begin now to act with faith and purpose.

Do all the work you can do, every day, and do each piece of work in a perfectly successful manner. Have the purpose to get rich, and put the power of success, in everything that you do. But do not do this merely with the idea of cultivating favor with your employer, in the hope that they, or those above you, will see your good work and advance you; it is not likely that they will do so.

The individual who is merely a "good" worker, filling their place to the very best of their ability, and is satisfied with that, is valuable to their employer. It is not to the employer's interest to promote them; they are indeed worth more where they are.

> *The person who is certain to advance is the one who is too big for their place, AND who has a clear concept of what they want to be – who knows that they can become what they want to be – who is determined to BE what they want to be.*

To secure advancement, something more is necessary than to be too large for your place. The person who is certain to advance is the one who is too big for their place, AND who has a clear concept of what they want to be – who knows that they can become what they want to be – who is determined to BE what they want to be.

Do not try to more than fill your present place with a view to pleasing your employer; do it with the idea of advancing yourself. Hold the faith and purpose of increase during work hours, after work hours, and before work hours. Hold it in such a way that every person who comes in contact with you, whether foreman, fellow worker, or social acquaintance, will feel the power of purpose radiating from you. Everyone will get the sense of and increase advancement from you. People will be attracted to you, and if there is no possibility for advancement in your present job, you will very soon see an opportunity to take another job.

People will be so attracted to you that you may find, as we have, that when you enter a place of business, such as a grocery store or gas station, with little traffic flow, that "hordes" of people will go into that store within a couple of minutes of you being there. You will then see the Law of Increase in action!

There is nothing in your circumstances or in the business situation that can keep you down. If you cannot get rich as an executive in big business, you can get rich driving a truck. If you begin to move in the Certain Way, you will certainly escape from the "clutches" of big business and get on to owning your own business, or wherever else you wish to be and do.

If a few thousands of its employees would enter upon the Certain Way, big business would soon be in a bad way. They would have to give

> *It is inherent in the Constitution of the Cosmos that: all things will be made available to you, and will work together for your good.*

their workers more opportunity, or go out of business. Nobody has to work for a conglomerate; they can keep people in so-called hopeless conditions only so long as there are individuals who are too ignorant to know of *The Science of Getting Rich*, or too intellectually lazy to practice it.

SUMMARY

There is a Power which never fails to present opportunity to the Advancing Human who is moving in obedience to law. God cannot help helping you, if you act in the Certain Way. The Infinite must do so in order to help Itself.

Begin this Certain Way of thinking and acting, and your faith and purpose will make you quick to see any opportunity to better your condition. Such opportunities will speedily come, for the Supreme, working in All, and working for you, will bring them before you.

Do not wait for the perfect opportunity. When an opportunity to be more than you are now is presented, and you feel impelled toward it, take it. It will be the first step toward a greater opportunity.

There is no such thing possible in this Universe as a lack of opportunities if you are living the advancing life. It is inherent in the *Constitution of the Cosmos that*: all things will be made available to you, and will work together for your good. You must certainly get rich if you act and think in the Certain Way. So let wage-earning men and women study this book with great care, and enter with confidence upon the course of action it prescribes; it will not fail.

CHAPTER SIXTEEN

THE WHOLE OF ABUNDANT LIVING

*M*any people will mock the idea that there is an exact science of getting rich. Holding the opinion that the supply of wealth is limited, they will insist that social and governmental institutions must be changed before even any considerable number of people can master their circumstances.

But this is not true.

It is true that existing governments keep the masses in poverty, but this is because the masses do not think and act in the Certain Way. If the masses begin to move forward as suggested in this book, neither governments nor industrial systems can stop them — all systems will have to be modified to accommodate the forward movement.

If the people have the *Advancing Mind*, have the *faith* that they can become rich, and move forward with the fixed *purpose* to become rich, nothing can keep them in poverty.

Individuals may enter upon the Certain Way at any time, and under any government, and make themselves rich. When any considerable number of individuals do so under any government, they will cause the system to be so modified as to open the way for others. The more people who get rich on the competitive plane, the worse for others; *the more who get rich on the creative plane, the better for others.*

The economic salvation of the masses can only be accomplished by getting a large number of people to become rich, by practicing the scientific method set down in this book. These will show others the way, and inspire them with a *desire* for real life, with the *faith* that it can be attained, and with the *purpose* to attain it.

For the present, however, it is enough to know that neither the government under which you live nor the capitalistic or competitive system of industry can keep you from getting rich. When you enter upon the creative plane of thought, you will rise above all these things and become a citizen of another kingdom.

But remember that your thought must be held upon the creative plane. You are never for an instant to be fooled into regarding the supply as limited, nor into acting on the amoral level of competition. Whenever you do fall into old ways of thought, correct yourself instantly, for when you are in the competitive mind, you have lost the cooperation of the Mind of the Whole.

Do not spend any time in planning as to how you will meet possible emergencies in the future. Except as the necessary policies may affect your actions today, you are only concerned with doing today's work in a perfectly successful manner, and not with emergencies which may arise tomorrow — you can attend to them as they come. Do not concern yourself with questions as to how you will overcome obstacles which may loom upon your business horizon, unless you can see plainly that your course must be altered today in order to avoid them.

No matter how great an obstruction may appear at a distance, you will find that if you go on in the Certain Way, it will disappear as you approach it — or that a way over, through, or around it will appear.

No possible combination of circumstances can defeat a man or woman who is proceeding to get rich along strictly scientific lines. No man or woman who obeys the law can fail to get rich, any more than one can multiply two by two and fail to get four.

Do not worry over possible disasters, obstacles, or unfavorable circumstances. There is time enough to meet such things when and if they present themselves to you in the immediate present. You will find that every difficulty carries with it the wherewithal for its overcoming.

Guard your speech. Never speak of yourself, your affairs, or of anything else in a discouraged or discouraging way. Never admit the possibility of failure, or speak in a way that implies failure as a possibility.

Never speak of the times as being hard, or of business conditions as being doubtful. Times may be hard and business doubtful for those who are on the competitive plane, but they can never be so for you — you can create what you want, and you are above fear! When others are having hard times and poor business, you will find your greatest opportunities.

Train yourself to think of and to look upon the world as a thing which is Becoming, which is growing; and to regard the seemingly corrupt as that which is only *undeveloped*. Always speak in terms of advancement; to do otherwise is to deny your faith, and to deny your faith is to lose it.

Never allow yourself to feel disappointed. You may expect to have a certain thing at a certain time, and not get it at that time; and this will appear to you like failure. But if you hold to your faith you will find that the failure is transparent. Go on in the Certain Way, and if you do not receive that thing, you will receive something so

> ... *keep your faith, hold to your purpose, have gratitude, and do, every day, all that can be done that day, doing each separate act in a successful manner.*

much better that you will see that the seeming failure was really a great success.

A student of this science had set his mind on making a certain business combination which seemed very desirable at the time, and he worked for weeks to bring it about. When the crucial time came, the thing failed in a perfectly inexplicable way. It was as if some unseen influence had been working secretly against him. He was not disappointed; on the contrary, he thanked God that his desire had been *overruled*, and went steadily on with a grateful mind. In a few weeks, an opportunity so much better came his way that he would not have made the first deal on any account. He saw that a Mind which knew more than he knew had prevented him from losing the greater good by entangling himself with the lesser.

That is the way every seeming failure will work out for you: if you keep your faith, hold to your purpose, have gratitude, and do, every day, all that can be done that day, doing each separate act in a successful manner.

When you make a failure, it is because you have not asked for enough! Keep on, and a larger thing than you were seeking will certainly come to you. Remember this.

You will not fail because you lack the necessary talent to do what you wish to do. If you go on as we have directed, you will develop all the talent that is necessary to your work. It is not within the scope of this book to deal with the science of cultivating talent; but it is as certain and simple as the process of getting rich.

However, do not hesitate or waver for fear that when you come to a certain challenge, you will fail for lack of ability; keep right on, and when you come to that challenge, the ability will be furnished to you. The same Source of ability which enabled the self-taught Abraham Lincoln to do the greatest work in government ever accomplished by a single human is open to you. You may draw upon all the Mind there is for wisdom to use in meeting the responsibilities which are laid upon you. Go on in full confidence.

Study this book. Make it your constant companion until you have mastered all the ideas contained in it. While you are getting firmly established in this faith, you will advance more steadily if you give up most recreations and pleasures; and stay away from places where ideas conflicting with these are espoused in lectures or sermons. Do not read pessimistic or conflicting literature, or get into arguments upon the matter. Do not listen to music, or watch TV programs, or listen to radio talk shows which depict decreasing contrary opinions. Spend most of your leisure time in contemplating your vision, and in cultivating gratitude, and in reading this book. It contains all you need to know of *The Science of Getting Rich*. You will find all the essentials condensed in the final summary.

SUMMARY

TRUTHS TO
THE SCIENCE OF GETTING RICH

1. There is a Thinking Stuff from which all things are made, and which, in its original state, permeates, penetrates, and fills the interspaces of the Universe.

2. A thought in this Substance, produces the thing that is imaged by that thought.

3. You can form things in your thoughts, and, by impressing your thoughts upon Formless Substance, can cause the thing you think about to be created.

4. In order to do this, you must pass from the competitive to the creative mind; otherwise you cannot be in harmony with the Formless Intelligence, which is always creative and never competitive in spirit.

5. You may come into full harmony with the Formless Substance by entertaining a lively and sincere gratitude for the blessings It bestows upon you. Gratitude unifies your mind with the Intelligence of Substance, so that your thoughts are received by the Formless.

You can remain upon the creative plane only by uniting yourself with the Formless Intelligence through a deep and continuous feeling of gratitude.

6. You must form a clear and definite mental picture of the things you want to do, or to become; and you must hold this mental image in your thoughts, while being deeply grateful to the Supreme that all your desires are being granted. You who wish to get rich must spend your leisure hours in contemplating your Vision and in earnest thanksgiving, that the reality is coming into being.

7. Too much emphasis cannot be given to the importance of frequent contemplation of the mental image, coupled with unwavering FAITH and devout GRATITUDE. This is the process by which the impression is given to the Formless, and the creative forces are set in motion.

8. The creative energy works through the established channels of natural growth, and of the industrial, political, and social order. All that is included in your mental image will

surely be brought to you if you follow the instructions previously given, and if you have unwavering FAITH. What you want will come to you through the ways of established trade and commerce.

9. In order to receive your image in reality, you must be ACTIVE. You must more than fill your present place. You must keep in mind the PURPOSE to get rich through the realization of your mental image. And you must do, every day, all that can be done that day, taking care to do each act in an efficient, successful manner. You must give to every person a use value in excess of the cash value you receive, so that each transaction makes for more life – and you must so hold the Advancing Thought that the impression of Increase will be communicated to all with whom you come in contact.

10. If you practice the foregoing instructions you will certainly get rich. And the riches you receive will be in exact proportion to the definiteness of your VISION, the firmness of your PURPOSE, the steadiness of your FAITH, and the depth of your GRATITUDE.

WALLACE WATTLES

*W*allace Wattles spent his entire life working out the principles and methods of the science outlined in this book. Through trial and error and much study and thought, he honed and polished his methods, and in the final years of his life, using these principles and actions, he began to manifest abundance.

Born in the late 1800's, the major portion of his life was cursed by poverty and the fear of poverty. Writes his daughter Florence, "He was always scheming and planning to get for his family those things which make the abundant life possible. Through it all, never for a moment did he lose confidence in the power of the Master Intelligence to right every wrong, and to give to every man and woman his or her share of the good things in life."

Florence continues, "He wrote almost constantly... in his later years. It was then that he formed his mental picture. He saw himself as a successful writer, a personality of power, an advancing man, and he began to work toward the realization of this vision... He lived every page of his books *(The Science of Getting Rich, The Science of Becoming Excellent, and The Science of Well Being).* In the last three years he made lots of money, and had good health except for his extreme frailty. In the last three years, my father made lots of money, and had good health except for his extreme frailty. His life was truly THE POWERFUL LIFE."

Wattles was a pioneer, and like the early trappers, he blazed the trails which became the freeways, in this case, to riches.

DR. JUDITH POWELL

*D*r. Judith Powell knows that your real treasure lies hidden within, and she has shared her secrets with thousands in the U.S.A., Europe and the Orient.

An internationally sought-after authority and speaker on expanding human excellence, Judith has written definitive articles for business and the general community on numerous enlightening topics. She has also co-authored the self-improvement book, *Silva Mind Mastery For The '90s*, distributed worldwide and translated into twelve languages. She is currently writing *A Date With Destiny*, a book on universal truths.

As one of the world's leading human potential lecturers and trainers, Dr. Judith Powell's popular motivational seminars include: Color Dynamics, Loving Yourself, Discover Your Perfect Mate, An Introduction to Neuro Linguistic Programming, and Silva Mind Mastery.

After receiving her Bachelor's Degree in Color Design and Business at Marygrove College in Michigan, she earned her Master's and Doctorate Degrees in Psychorientology at the Institute of Psychorientology, Texas, as well as Masters and Trainers Certifications in Neuro Linguistic Programming (the language of the brain).

Judith, an award-winning TV host for "It's All In Your Mind," also directs, along with her husband, Dr. Tag Powell, three companies in St. Petersburg, Florida, where they also live with their three Scottish Terriers — Master, Buddha, and Isis.